Rune R

Wisdom and (
for
the Life Journey

Ruarik Grimnisson

Capall Bann Publishing

www.capallbann.co.uk

Rune Rede
Wisdom and Magick for the Life Journey

©2001 Ruarik Grimnisson

ISBN 186163 1081

ALL RIGHTS RESERVED

Camera-ready copy was prepared by the author.

Cover design by Paul Mason

Published by:

Capall Bann Publishing

Freshfields

Chieveley

Berks

RG20 8TF

Tel/Fax 00 44 1635 247050

www.capallbann.co.uk

"... At night in hall   the norns did come
to the lord they alloted   his life and orlog:
to him awarded   under welkin most fame,
under heaven to be   among heroes first.

His fate-thread span they   to o'erspread the world
for Borghild's bairn   in Bralund castle;
they gathered together   the golden threads,
an in moon-hall's middle   they made them fast."
(The first lay of Helgi the Hunding-slayer - Poetic Edda)

"And if it is true that we acquired our knowledge before
our birth,
and lost it at the moment of birth, but afterward,
by the exercise of our senses upon sensible objects,
recover the knowledge which we had once before,
I suppose that what we call learning will be
the recovery of our own knowledge ..."
(Plato)

Dedication

To my beloved sons Kurt and Khem who have made
this life journey worthwhile.

REYN TIL RUNA

Preface

This book has been written in answer to the increasing demand for traditional Rune Lore. There are many books on the market pertaining to Runes but not all of them are founded on ancient tradition. Those on Rune Lore fall basically into three categories; Academic, Religious/Magickal and New Age. It can be difficult for those who are new to these studies to decipher where one category ends and another begins.

Academic research lays the historical foundation for knowledge of the Runic Culture; and our Northern forebears' society was indeed magickal. The natural and supernatural worlds intertwined with their social world. They were not separated from the realities of physical and spiritual life by the technological comforts and mental placebos that we, as modern folk, now take for granted.

The current trend among many New Age writers of Rune Lore, especially those with a strong Universalist agenda, is to negate historical reality and to re-interpret the Runes according to popular philosophical and socio-political ideology, even to the point of ignoring textual and archaeological evidence. In some cases, they have even made up their own rune staves (glyphs or symbols) and given them artificial meaning and commentary. This does a grave disservice to our heritage and to those who wish to draw on the wisdom of the ancestors.

This book is the product of 14 years of research and practical experimentation. I have been asked on many occasions to recommend Rune books. I have done so but what is often asked of me is the whereabouts of books that don't try to tell you everything; books that don't expect you to be a boffin to read them; books that don't lead you down the garden path into New Age fantasy. I have tried to fill this gap with this current volume.

This book incorporates the essentials that are common to those cultures where Runes were used, and remains true to their Heathen origins. The ways of Rune working have evolved over centuries but the essential symbolism, as a key to understanding the profound mysteries of existence, is just as relevant today, as it was to our ancestors.

It is important to remember that the Runic 'alphabets' were not just a system of writing for the Germanic peoples - they were a Life-Code. Encrypted in their numerical ordering and individual symbolism is a guide to the life journey of the soul - a holistic approach for the individual and collective folk to survive and thrive in the worlds of nature, mankind and the spiritual realms. Their magick arose from the understanding of the inseparability of all phenomena - what our ancestors called the Wyrd.

I have presented an integrated collection of basic Rune Lore, I trust, in the manner it was meant to be given - as a counsel for the soul's life journey. The Old English word for counsel is "Red"- Rede, hence the title of this book. I have used the collective system of the twenty four rune staves known as the "Elder Futhark", they being the oldest complete runic system yet found.

This book is both concise and precise, not pretending to be an atlas of the Runic World, but a traveller's pocket guide. It contains the codes that will make the way clear. It has been designed as a ready reference, not only for those who wish to explore the patterns of Wyrd, but for those who seek essential reference to the power of the Runes, manifested and unmanifested. For those who are seeking insight into the psychological world of our pre-industrial ancestors, this book will reveal to you their basic attitudes and expectations. The ancestral mythology interwoven with each rune-rede is presented for you own contemplation. It is my experience that most people begin their exploration of the runic world with the use of rune staves for divination - seeking their rede (counsel). Their divinatory task is not fortune telling. It is to unlock self knowledge, provide profound insight, and hopefully encourage the development of wisdom, which in turn will stimulate the need to make the most out of your life - your "will to power".

Study of the knowledge herein seen through the lens of heathen understanding will reveal an alternative map of reality that will aid you on your life journey.

For the student of the Occult, it will serve as a stimulant for deeper mystical studies.

May it serve you well.

Ruarik Grimnisson

Port Macquarie, Australia, 2001.

Acknowledgements

I wish to thank the following folk whose support and inspiration made this book possible. Katherine Elliot, Lisa Scarrott, Stephen Plowright, GeirR and Eyestein Fokstuen and especially Edred Thorsson, Runemaster; the kin of the Rune-Gild, the Assembly of the Elder Troth and the Rune-Net.

Artists - Annika Robertson (Illustrations & Rune Graphics).
Gregory Griffith (Borders & Chapter Terminator).

Translations - The Old English, Old Icelandic Rune Poems and the Old Norse Rune Rhymes are original translations by Daniel Bray.

Reference

Lee M. Hollander's translations of stanzas from the Poetic Edda used in this book as chapter leaders and elsewhere.

Marijane Osborn and Stella Longland's translations of excerpts from the Havamal (Poetic Edda).

James A. Chisolm's translations from various Sagas dealing with Seith.

M. Magnusson and H. Palsson's translation of the excerpt from Njal's Saga.

Translations of the Old Norse, Old English and Old Saxon languages are mostly by the authors of the source material (see Book Hoard). Where neccesary, I have provided my own interpretations of same. Many source words (see glossary) have been modernised for ease of pronunciation.

Gain they who grasp them
Happy they who heed them!
(The Sayings of Har - Poetic Edda)

Foreword

Rune Rede is structured to guide readers on an easy path of information gathering and practical applications. Its lore extends from the earliest period of rune usage to the present.

The journey begins with the Introduction – The Elder Futhark, with a visit to the oldest recorded rune system of the Germanic culture used by the mysterious masters of lore and magick – the gift of Odinn.

Then we panoramically walk through the historic valley of the runic world in chapter one – A Brief History of the Runes, to review the development and dispersal of rune lore from ancient origins to modern reconstruction.

From this platform we soar, in chapter two - The Nine Worlds, through mysterious dimensions parallel, and accessible, to our own which are inhabited by gods, elves, dwarfs, giants and supernatural beasts. Wondrous tales of description are sung to us through the ancient myths of the Nordics.

In chapter three – Soul Lore, we explore the multi-faceted nature of our being – its make up and qualities both mortal and transcendental, as revealed to us by our ancestral and present day mystics, magicians and healers.

We have explained to us in chapter four – Time and Probability, the ancient concepts of synchronicity in relation to our perception of reality and the secrets of using our will to influence life changes.

In chapter five - Divination, we peer into the reflective waters of consciousness that show us methods of perceiving events and their meanings within the multiverse of existence.

Now deeper into the mountains we hike in chapter six – The Runic Code, to be given the key to unlock the arcane wisdom chest of runic correspondence, numerical connectivity and primal laws that shape the lives and rebirths of all entities.

Into the hall of the lore masters we gather, in chapter seven – Freyja's Aett, chapter eight - Hagal's Aett and chapter nine – Tyr's Aett, to focus ourselves in concentrated study of the twenty four runes of the Elder Futhark. We are given their associated mythology, correspondences, divinatory meanings and detailed pragmatic counsel.

In chapter ten – Crafting Your Own Runes, we venture into the woods and workshop to be taught ways of choosing the best materials and methods to handcraft, and magickally prepare, our own set of rune staves.

Seating ourselves quietly within a dappled forest clearing, in chapter eleven – Preparation for Casting, we practice the arcane methods of tuning our beings into the web of existence. We contact our inner selves and connect with the numinous forces in readiness for our divination.

In chapter twelve – Casting and Reading the Runes, we are shown various methods, with examples, to enable us to practice a wide range of divinatory techniques to investigate the hidden patterns, to our advantage, of the internal and external worlds of reality.

The last lesson from our wisdom warders, chapter thirteen – Magickal Applications of the Runes, is the secret lore of applied rune magick. Not only is it useful to gather power for the journeyman but it can stimulate self-actualisation, through discipline and trust, for every one who seeks greater control of their own destiny.

The Appendix invites us to review the historical rune system variations, other than the Elder Futhark, that developed within the far flung tribes of the runic culture. Ranging from the Anglo-Saxon times, through the Viking Age, to 20th century Germany – their staves, origins, lore and meanings.

The Glossary provides an instant reference for all names and terms – their meanings, origins and associations - used throughout this journeyman's handbook.

The Bookhoard, besides being a record of references used for Rune Rede, is a valuable resource for those wishing to discover more about the profound ancestral wisdom that is embodied in the runes.

The Author

List of Abbreviations

BCE	Before the Common Era (= B.C.)
CE	Common Era (= A.D.)
F	Frisian
OE	Old English
OERP	Old English Rune Poem
ME	Modern English
ON	Old Norse
OS	Old Saxon

Prounciation Notes

Many source words used in this book have been modernised, while retaining some common Germanic phonetic values:

a	as in "cart"
à	as in "lather"
e	as in "pen"
è	as in *ay* in "day"
i	as in "pin"
ì	as *ee* in "meet"
o	as in "open"
u	as in "put"
ù	as in "rule'
æ	or 'ae' as *ai* in "fair"
œ	or 'oe' as *u* in "fur"
ei	as in *ay* in "pay" or *i* in "line"
j	as *y* in "year"
dh	as in *th* in "the"
th	as in *th* in "thing"
r	at the end of a word is silent

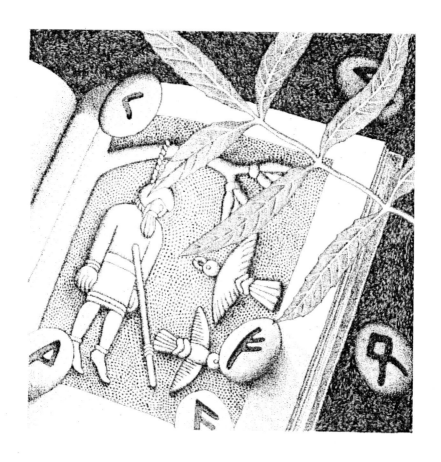

Table of Contents

Introduction
The Elder Futhark

Then gathered together the gods for counsel,
the Holy hosts,   and held converse;
to night and new moon their   names they gave,
the morning named, and midday also,
forenoon and evening, to order the year.

(The Prophecy of the Seeress-Poetic Edda)

18

Introduction
The Elder Futhark

In magickal and mythological tradition, the origin of the
Runes goes back to (Odin) Odhinn, the All-Father of the
Germanic Gods. He is also known as Wotan, Wodan and
Woden. In the Icelandic collection of poetry known as the
"Poetic Edda", Odhinn himself says:

I wot that I hung   on the wind-tossed tree
all of nights nine,
wounded by spear, bespoken to Odhinn
bespoken myself to myself,
upon that tree of which none telleth
from what roots it doth rise.

Neither horn they upheld   nor handed me bread
I looked down below me -
aloud I cried -
caught up the runes, caught them up wailing,
thence to the ground fell again.

(The Sayings of Har - Poetic Edda, trans. by Lee M. Hollander)

This describes a shamanistic initiation on "The World Tree" -
known as "Yggdrasil" (Steed of the Terrible One) which is the
axis of the Multiverse known as the Nine Worlds. Travelling
through these worlds in search of knowledge and finally into
the realm of death; Rune (secret) wisdom etched into his
being, Odhinn returns to the world of living at a cost of great
suffering.

He gives the Divine gift - the Rune Staves - keys to the secrets in a communicable form, to the Middle-World dwellers (Midgard) - Mankind. The 24 runes are divided into three sets of eight (known as Aettir (ON) ie. families) and a name of a god or goddess is given to designate each Aett . This is taken from the sound of the first stave of each row of eight. The names given for each are a reconstruction in the earliest Proto-Germanic form.

The Elder Futhark

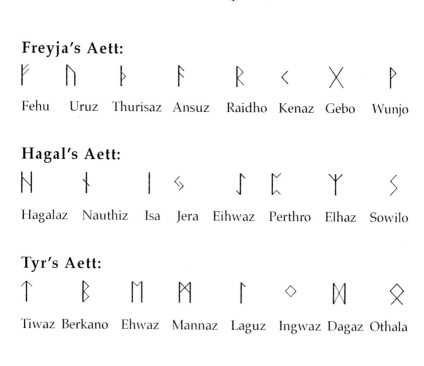

Freyja's Aett:

Fehu   Uruz   Thurisaz   Ansuz   Raidho   Kenaz   Gebo   Wunjo

Hagal's Aett:

Hagalaz   Nauthiz   Isa   Jera   Eihwaz   Perthro   Elhaz   Sowilo

Tyr's Aett:

Tiwaz   Berkano   Ehwaz   Mannaz   Laguz   Ingwaz   Dagaz   Othala

This is their original order, but note the position of the last two staves in Tyr's Aett may be inter-changed. Archaeological examples of both stave positions have been unearthed.

20

In the *Havamal* (Sayings of Har), part of the Icelandic medieval text known as the Poetic Edda, from which the above quote is taken, Odhinn continues with his tale of the gaining of the runes. He says that he received "nine powerful songs" - charms called Rune Galdar, *Galdr* (ON) - from his maternal grandfather a giant named Bolthor (evil thorn). These rune songs (Galdar) were powerful magickal spells that enabled Odhinn to gain possession, from the giants, of the Mead of Poetry (inspiration) which was brewed from the blood of the being named Kvasir (wise one?).

After the primal war between the gods of thought/intellect (the Aesir) and the gods of instinct/nature(the Vanir) a peace pact was made and sealed by both parties spitting into a cauldron. This spittle fermented into a Being of Wisdom - Kvasir. Two Dwarfs Fjalarr (deceiver) and Galarr (screamer) were envious of his wisdom and the attention he attracted so they slew him and magickally brewed his blood into mead which became known as 'the mead of inspiration'. The giant Suttung (sup-heavy) claimed the mead as compensation for the murder of his parents by this evil pair - but boasted to all and sundry of his magickal brew. He sealed it in the three cauldrons called Odroerir (frenzy stirrer), Bodn (vessel) and Son (blood). It was secreted inside a mountain named Hnitborg (crashing rock) within Jotunheim (home of the giants) and guarded by his daughter Gunnlod (war summons).

Odhinn searching in his disguise of Bolverkr (evil doer) tricked Suttung's brother Baugi (bowed) into drilling a hole in the base of the mountain. He turned himself into a snake and entered. Then he transformed himself into a one-eyed giant and seduced Gunnlod over three days and nights. He asked for three draughts of the mead as a reward for his virile efforts. She couldn't refuse him and with each draught he emptied one of the three kettles. Odhinn then changed himself into a huge eagle and flew back to Asgard. As he was being hastily pursued by Suttung also in eagle form, a little of the mead spilled from his beak during the journey and fell to Midgard. After regurgitating the mead into awaiting crocks, he drank a draught and he discovered within himself nine more charms of power. It is said that Odhinn occasionally offers Kvasir's blood to favoured humans.

In the *Vafthrudnismal* (Sayings of Vathrudnir), also a part of the Poetic Edda, Odhinn enters a competition of wits with the giant Vathrudnir (mighty weaver). During the exchange the giant reveals to Odhinn that he is able to read the runes of the giants and of the gods because he has visited all the worlds including the land of the dead.

In the *Havamal*, Odhinn says that runes were also given to Dainn (dead) for the Elves, to Dvalinn (dawdler) for the Dwarves and to Asvithr or Alsvinn (all swift) for the Giants.

Chapter six, The Runic Code, explores numerological lore and leads to the chapters on the Aettir (the rune staves) which reveals the evolution of their primal energies on a mythological, natural, social and personal level. The Rune Rede given with each stave allows self-contained reference to the meaning of the rune and its application to you at the time of consultation.

The meanings and associations given to each rune stave have been focused to stimulate your intellect and intuition regarding the exoteric and esoteric mystery of each stave and their collective pattern. This book has been structured for easy absorption of knowledge. To get the most from it, I recommend you start at the beginning as each chapter lays the foundation for the next.

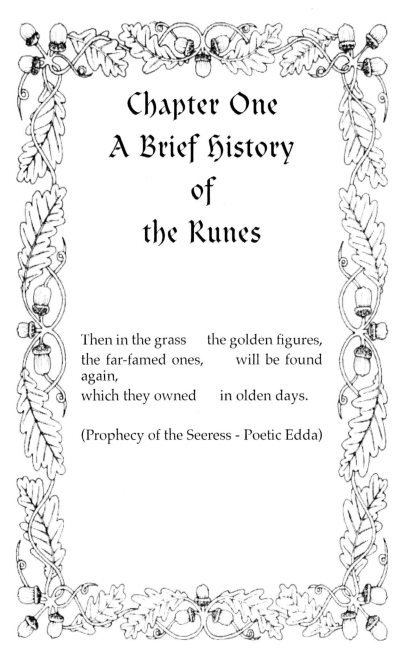

Chapter One
A Brief History
of
the Runes

Then in the grass   the golden figures,
the far-famed ones,   will be found
again,
which they owned   in olden days.

(Prophecy of the Seeress - Poetic Edda)

Chapter One
A Brief History of the Runes

The word Rune, Rûn (OE), Rùn (ON) means mystery, secret: council and lore, magical sign and written characters. Its Proto-Indo-European roots give it the meanings of "to roar and to whisper" - incantation; and "magical binding".

We know that the Germanic people became a folk distinct from their Indo-European forebears by the 2nd Millennium BCE - the European Bronze Age, sharing the North, North-West and Central Europe with the Celts (who shared a root word for rune - *runo* - with the Germanics). The pre-history of the runes can be traced back to the ideographic cult symbols (or Sigils) found in Northern Europe, incised in rock, dating from Neolithic times, and common to many branches of European Culture.

The runes, as we know them, had their origin after the Indo-European dispersal and language separations. Certain cult symbols may have been given distinctive phonetic values peculiar to the Germanic folk. There is no surviving archaeological evidence that the runes existed in their present form before the middle Iron Age. However, they were probably in use by about 200 BCE when carving on wood was the preferred medium for the inscription. Around 200 CE, the Elder Futhark was recorded for posterity on a metal helmet. It consisted of 24 runes. Runes were traditionally carved in wood or stone although bone and metal were also used when appropriate for particular magickal requirements.

The word Futhark comes from the sound representation of the first six staves: F,U,Th,A,R,K, much in the same way as the word 'alphabet' comes from the sound of the first two letters

25

of the Greek alphabet: Alpha and Beta. Initially, Rune lore was passed down orally. The staves were used to represent each mystery. They embodied the esoteric law attached to each symbol and were not originally used for common communication, but kept for magickal purposes.

The Runic Lore-Warders were the custodians of ancient knowledge. They were the intellectual and religious leaders of their culture. Through migration from the North and East and the searching for trade, the Germanic tribes eventually re-established contact with other branches of the Indo-European peoples, who had retained variants of common ancestral symbols.

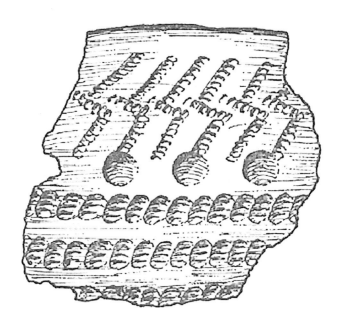

Comb Pottery Piece, 2000 BCE, Norway. Markings are similar to later runes.

Rock carvings, Bronze Age, Hallristninga, Sweden.

Through their contact with the Etruscans (northern Italy), Romans and Greeks (whose alphabet shows the greatest similarity to the Rune Staves), the Germanic tribes may have synthesised their own cult sigils and staves with these alphabets. The purpose being to retain the ancient Indo-European inheritance, and express the evolution of their magickal knowledge. They created a new meta-language - a way of enhancing communication between the worlds of humans, spirits and Gods. The Roman historian Tacitus recorded observations of Germanic rune casting rituals in the 1st century (98 CE). See chapter five; Divination.

It has been suggested that the Germanic tribe called the Heruli who wandered extensively - acting as mercenaries throughout the Roman Empire until the 6th century CE - may have been responsible for collating and transmitting much of the rune lore between the separated Germanic tribes. Unfortunately the Heruli allowed themselves to be divided when half the tribe became Christian while the remainder stayed Heathen. The Christian's fought a war on Rome's behalf against their Heathen kin, who refused to live under Christian-Roman domination, resulting in the decimation of the Heruli as a tribal entity.

Bone Piece, 8th Century, Derbyshire, England

Over time, two major variants of the Futhark arose. On the Continent, the tribes of Angles and Frisians, who intermingled, adapted the runes to their language system. With the great migrations of Germanic tribes to the British Isles - Angles, Saxons, Jutes and Frisians - and the absorbed Celtic peoples - adapted the runes to accommodate the sound changes in their combined dialects. This occurred around the fifth century CE bringing the 24 runes of the Elder Futhark (or Common Germanic Futhark) to 29 (called the Anglo-Frisian Furthorc). These were later increased, by four more runes from Northumbria, to 33 - collectively called the Anglo-Saxon Futhorc.

In Scandinavia, the Futhark did not change until the eighth century. Again this was the result of linguistic changes. The rune tally was reduced to 16 but the magickal order and combination was kept through integrating the functions of certain runes for multiple meaning. This was called the Younger Futhark.

The Viking invasions and migrations throughout northern Europe and the British Isles from the late 8th century till the middle of the 11th regenerated rune lore among the Germanic tribes but also led to variations of the runic script particularly the Younger Futhark.

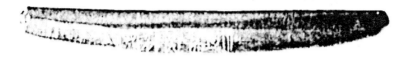

Yew Wand, ca. 800CE, Westeremden, Frisia.

By the end of the Viking age (the 12th Century CE), this system had been corrupted through contact with the Latin alphabetical order. By this time, Christianity had become the State religion of Europe; Sweden, in Scandinavia, being the last heathen outpost to succumb.

The Christian Church and its State extensions enacted laws to suppress rune knowledge, even to the point of instigating a death penalty for heathen magickal usage - inscription, and utterance. But the Runes themselves survived through the agency of monks, scholars, poets, magicians, craftsmen and the common people. Runes were still toleated for funerary inscriptions, memorial stones and messages within Scandinavia and the British Isles. In England, towards the end of the first millennium, the monks transcribed what we now call the *Old English Rune Poems* (originally recorded in the 8th - 9th century CE) albeit somewhat disguised by a thin Christian overlay.

In the 12th - 13th Century European monks recorded what is known as the *Old Norse Rune Songs*. The *Old Icelandic Rune Poems* were transcribed in the 17th century. Protected by their position, many European aristocrats saw themselves as guardians of their ancient heritage. In Iceland and Denmark from the 11th - 15th Centuries, history, mythology, poetry, calendars and sagas were written, copied and annotated;

29

Inscription from a magickal ring, 8th-9th century, England.

thus preserving knowledge of the pre-Christian culture.

The Gothic revival began in Sweden in the 16th - 17th century exemplified by such great men as Johann Magnus, the first "high priest" of Gothicism and last Roman Catholic Bishop of Uppsala, Sweden (site of the last heathen temple to succumb to Christianity in 1100 CE) and Johannes Bureus, tutor and adviser of king Gustavus Adolphus of Sweden. Bureus recorded the runic inscriptions throughout the country and was the first Renaissance scholar to decipher their meaning. He is considered one of the fathers of modern academic runology along with his contemporary, Ole Worm of Denmark.

The 19th century saw the English and German Romantic (or German-tic!) movement where the folk once again looked to their own culture for inspiration rather than the Mediterranean. In the first half of the century Jacob and Willhelm Grimm published volumes on Teutonic Mythology and collections of Folk (fairy) Tales and in the latter half Richard Wagner produced great works of music based on the ancient Germanic myths and legends.

Other high profile personalities such as England's William Morris rekindled the fire of ancient interest with his works of historical and mythological translations and revival of traditional crafts. Art, music, operas and works of literary fiction inspired by new archaeological discoveries flourished in European Society. Political movements arose propelled by the momentum of the past.

In the late 19th and early 20th century, the Germans continued to explore the heritage. An 18-rune system was synthesised by Guido Von List. This is known as the Armanen Futhark (or the

Armanen Runes), and is still used by modern German Magicians. Unfortunately, the National Socialist Party tried to appropriate the runes for their own political posturing, whilst eliminating many who would not sell out to bigotry; by murder and concentration camp internment.

After World War Two there was a renewed interest by European Academics, Linguists and Historians. Gradually the emotional association with the totalitarian racists declined. The late 1960's and particularly the 1970's saw an upsurge of seekers for spiritual inspiration. Many looked not only to the Ancient East but to the Ancient North.

In the U.S.A Stephen A. MacNallen revived interest of the northern Folkways with the founding of the *Asatru Free Assembly* in 1972 and James A. Chisolm continued this momentum with the founding of the *Ring of Troth* in 1987. Stephen E. Flowers (a.k.a. Edred Thorsson) took rune lore out of the hallowed university halls with the founding of the *Rune-Gild* in 1988 which is now an international body with a world wide membership.

Since then a plethora of Northern Folkways Groups have been established throughout the British Isles, Europe and across the globe - wherever the descendents of the Germanic peoples have re-rooted themselves. Most recently a new world wide organisation - the *International Asatru & Odinic Alliance* - has risen to prominence. Italy has the *Comunita Odinista*. In the English speaking countries, the UK has the *Odinic Rite*; the USA has the *Asatru Folk Assembly* and the *Asatru Alliance*. Australia has the *Assembly of the Elder Troth*, the *Rune-Net* and the *Odinic Rite Australia*. New Zealand has the *Asatru Fellowship*. What they all have in common is the prominence of the study and application of Rune Lore.

Through the 1980's and '90's English authors such as Nigel Pennick, Tony Willis, Bernard King and Michael Howard found their once obscure knowledge to be of great interest to the Occult/New Age publishing houses. Brian Bates is renowned for his in-depth studies of our Anglo-Saxon ethnic spiritually. Stephan Grundy (a.k.a. Kveldulf Gundarsson) is a world renowned writer of rune lore and historical fiction. Diana L. Paxson writes on the ancient Germanic magickal craft of Seidhr (akin to Shamanism) as well as books of Celtic and Germanic historical fiction. One has only to go to their local book store to see an incredible range of books on runes and associated cultural studies.

The Classical Mediterranean cultures and philosophies of the Middle East may have come to dominate the appearance of Western Culture but behind this overlay are the Christian suppressed Heathen Traditions of the North. These stem back to the dim memories of the great migrations of the Neolithic peoples during the Post-Glacial period, 10,000 years ago and the more recent wave of Indo-Europeans 5000-4000 years ago.

The 1980's and 90's has seen a turbulent resurrection of ethnic (tribal) identity within the European Mega-State, journalistically called 'Balkanisation'. A sign of the resistance to a universal monoculture and a need for links with the past to give continuity into the future.

Organisations have arisen through out the world wherever the descendants of the Germanic Folk have spread offering affiliation to those who are interested in studying rune lore and other hereditary cultural traditions.

The original traditions are being revived through reconstruction. Every person who delves into these secrets can free themselves from ignorance and fulfil their birthright. Knowledge may come through words but wisdom only comes through practical application.

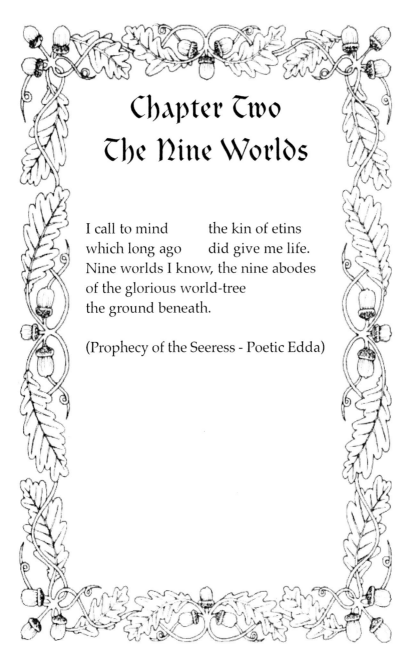

Chapter Two
The Nine Worlds

I call to mind   the kin of etins
which long ago   did give me life.
Nine worlds I know, the nine abodes
of the glorious world-tree
the ground beneath.

(Prophecy of the Seeress - Poetic Edda)

Chapter Two
The Nine Worlds

Knowledge of the Germanic Heathen Cosmology survived through the mythology of the Norse cultures. Compared with the straight forward triunal Christian Cosmology of Heaven, Earth and Hell, the Germanic model is intricate and elaborate - even to the point of complexity.

It has nine worlds of being all interconnected but self-contained dimensions. The worlds are populated by beings some of whom are unamicable to organic life and others who are essential for its well being. Some worlds are of matter while others are of anti-matter. Some worlds are of nature while others are of spirit. Even though the basic imagery is of a three tiered system with each tier consisting of three worlds with all being supported and penetrated by a central axis; these worlds though separate in time and space essentially co-exist unilaterally. These nine worlds are collectively called the Multiverse.

The central axis of the Multiverse is known as the World Tree and is called Yggdrasil (Ygg's Horse, ie. Odhinn's Steed), Irminsul (primal pillar) and Laeradr (counsel giver). Its roots rest in the trilevel Well of Wyrd (the container of all phenomena) which brings forth all manifestation in the Nine Worlds (see chapter four; Time and Probability).

Midgard was shaped by the gods Odhinn (inspiration), Vili (will) and Vè (self awareness?) who were the sons of Bor (son?) who was the son of Buri (son?) and Bestla (bark?) who was the daughter of Bolthor (evil thorn). Buri was shaped by the cow Audumla (fecund care?) from her licking of salty ice blocks. She in turn was formed from the ice thaw in the Ginnungagap (beguiling void) but before her existence, and also formed

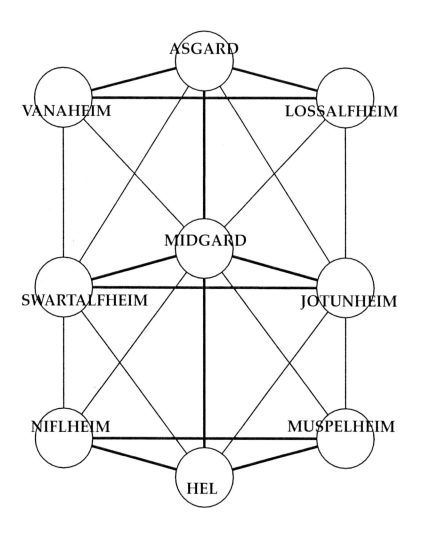

THE NINE WORLDS

from the condensing icy mist of this void, came the primal being, the first Frost-Giant called Ymir (groaner). He was formed when the heat of Muspellheim (see below) met the rime of Niflheim (see below) in the void of Ginnungagap melting the ice into drips which quickened with life. Audumla fed Ymir from her four teats. From his body oozed the race of Frost-giants.

Odhinn, Vili and Vè slew Ymir and dismembered him in the Ginnungagap. His blood caused a flood which drowned all the race of giants except for a male and female. From his flesh they shaped the earth; his unbroken bones formed the mountains. From the broken bones, his teeth and his fragmented jaw they shaped the boulders and rocks. His skull formed the vault of the sky which touched the four corners of the earth. From the maggots that infested his remains they shaped the race of Dwarfs and set four of them as supports under the points where the skull touched the earth. They named the dwarfs East and West, North and South. They then flung Ymir's brains into the sky to become the clouds. From his blood they fashioned the lakes and oceans. Then the three brothers seized sparks and embers from Muspellheim and cast them into the sky to become the Sun, Moon and Stars.

When all was in place, the three brothers fashioned the first man (Ask) and woman (Embla) from two fallen trees found on the seashore - man from the Ash tree, woman from the Elm tree. Odhinn breathed the life-spirit into them; Vili gave them wits and feelings; Vè gave them senses - hearing and sight.

Now back to the Nine World infrastructure. Within the top tier, the highest metaphysical realm, is **Asgard** (enclosure of the Ases) where dwell the Æsir in their halls - gods and goddesses of war, will and intelligence. They personify self-conscious and ordered evolution.

Also on this level is **Vanaheim** (home of flowing water) where dwell the Vanir in their halls - gods and goddesses of nature and fertility. They personify the survival instincts and evolution through natural selection. Vanaheim is said to be west of Midgard.

Lossàlfheim where dwell the Light Elves - shapers of thought and matter and warders of the natural world - is here too and is said to be easily accessible from Midgard. The Light Elves give their allegiance to Freyr who received their kingdom as a "Tooth Gift" from the Æsir (Álfheim - home of the Tooth Fairy?).

The Æsir and Vanir were once enemies and fought a fierce war when mankind was in its infancy. The Vanir won but offered peace to the Æsir who accepted. Hostages were exchanged until trust was built between them. They now are united and their functions are intertwined. The best known god/esses of Asgard are the Æsir - Odhinn, Frigga, Thorr and Loki; and among the Vanir - Njord, Jord, Freyja and Freyr. It is written that in Asgard there are twelve divine gods and twelve divine goddesses.

Within the next tier, and south of Asgard is **Midgard** (middle enclosure). This is the second highest metaphysical realm; the middle level inhabited by humanity. This realm is separated from the top tier and the one below it by many rivers and a vast ocean, made from Ymir's blood, which surrounds it but Asgard and Midgard are joined by a bridge of air, water and fire called Bifrost (shimmering path) or Asabrù (the bridge of the Ases). Within this ocean lives the terrible serpent called Jormungand (mighty wand) who encircles Midgard. He is so long that he bites on his own tail.

To the north-east of Midgard across a river and over towering mountains of ice and snow is **Jotunheim**, the home of the Giants - preconscious beings of [necessary] dissolution and chaos. On its common borders between Asgard and Midgard lies the forest called Jarnvidr (iron wood). Here lurks the mighty wolf Fenrir (fen dweller) who will slay Odhinn in the final battle called Ragnarok (destruction of the powers).

To the north-west of Midgard is **Svartàlfheim**, home of the Dark Elves or Dwarfs who are said to dwell in the mountains, grottos and underground caverns. They are shrewd beings and excellent smiths, shapers of power and form - emotions and matter - who produce items of wondrous magick that the gods covet and sometimes gain. Their leader is Modsognir (frenzy roarer) and his deputy is Durinn (sleepy).

Within the lowest metaphysical tier, but north of Midgard is **Niflheim** (mist home); the land of the dead - the souls unworthy to enter Asgard. It is described as a place of bitter cold, mist and unending night - ice and darkness.

Within this realm is **Hel** (concealed) which is not a place of eternal punishment but a place of rest for souls awaiting their rebirths into Midgard. Many of its halls are bright and warm where existence is not much different from Midgard but there is a hall of punishment for the wicked called Kvollheimr (home of twilight).

Hel and Asgard are connected by a bridge called Gjallabrù (resounding bridge). It can be reached from Midgard through the road called Helvegr (hellway) and is separated from the land of the living by the gate called Nàgrind (corpse gate).

Below Hel is the dark place called **Niflhel** (concealed mist) where the souls that are too evil to dwell in the halls of the goddess of the dead - Hella (concealer) - pass down into the final darkness to die a second death into oblivion. The serpent Nidhogg (vicious blow) consumes their subtle bodies. This same serpent gnaws on the roots of the World Tree.

Still within this tier and to the south of Asgard is **Muspellheim**, (home of doom?). It is a region of pure fire (possibly antimatter?). It is from this place that the 'sons of Muspell' - their ruler is the fire-being Surt (black-one) - fare forth to join in battle against Asgard's dwellers in the final conflict called Ragnarok (destruction of the powers) that will see the Nine Worlds destroyed (but not the World Tree). Muspellheim is separated from Asgard by the vast forest called Myrkvidhr (murk wood).

Chapter Three
Soul Lore

Cattle die   and kinsmen die
thyself eke soon wilt die
one thing, I wot,   will wither never
the doom over each one dead.

(The Sayings of Har - Poetic Edda)

42

Chapter Three
Soul Lore

Every culture has a representative structure of the relationship of spirit and matter.

The Germanic peoples understood the complexity of existence. Like many organic cultures, they had numerous words to represent fine shades of distinction between varieties of objects, concepts and experience. This was just as true for their religion called *Sede* (OS) or *Siðr* (ON), meaning Custom.

The term Soul Lore is appropriate; for the Germanic Heathen saw the soul as being composed of many parts interwoven in function. These aspects of consciousness taken as a whole would be termed the "Self".

This Self is the cohesion of all the qualities of body and spirit. For Self to function to its fullest, the person had to know by direct experience his own nature. The sense of unity or wholeness had to be won through great effort. The understanding of the mystery of existence was the aim of the rune worker. A basic awareness of the soul lore is needed by those who desire to get the most benefit from the study and use of the runes. The information we have was mainly record-ed by the Christian clergy in England, Germany, Scandinavia and Iceland.

The Old English called the immortal soul by the names of Ferth (*Feorh*) and Ghost (*Gàst*). The Ferth is all the nonphysical components of the psycho-somatic complex, excluding the Fetch, that survive the death of the body. It is the closest idea to the modern psychological concept of the self. The Ferth or Ghost has the ability while still embodied to perceive the other dimensions of the World Tree and can be sent 'faring forth' to visit these worlds (astral projection) although this function was considered dangerous - leaving the body unattended - and most usually the Fetch was employed for this purpose. The Ferth survives the death of the body. The term Ghost did not just mean a disembodied spirit but also the spirit within a living body. Hence we still use the term "give up the ghost" to refer to someone's death.

The use of the word soul declined in Heathen usage as it was adopted by the Christians to fit their theology. For the Soul, *Sāwol* (OE), in heathen lore referred to the mortal aspects of the psycho-somatic complex - those that perished with the body. The three main categories of the soul (as in the present day meaning of immortal spirit) are the Mind, the Memory and the Emotions. These also have sub-components (see below).

The Mind, *Mynd*(OE), contains personal memories of deeds, knowledge and wisdom, *Myne*(OE), along with ancestral memories and inherited instinct, *Orthanc* (OE). The ancestral memories are of actual deeds, lessons learned and errors made - the collective [folk] unconscious. The ancestral component is tied to the personal component by a bridging consciousness known as the Fetch, *Faecce* (OE) and *Fylgja* (ON) which connects the deeds of past lives, *Orlaw* (OE) and *Orlog* (ON), both personal and clanic with its manifestation - rewards waiting and debts to oblige - *Wyrd* (OE) and *Urdhr* (ON), in the present life of the person.

The underlying psychology of the Germanic Heathen was the drive to personally accumulate luck or Speed, *Spaed*(OE), and power or Main, *Maegen* (OE), as they were attached to the Ghost and could be drawn upon in this life and in the next rebirth. They were essential for success in any undertaking. Speed is the luck or power of the individual and has the same meaning as the Old Norse term *Hamingja* and was believed to be tied to the Fetch and determined by the Orlog. It was passed down through families or transferred to individuals by willing intent or magick.

So it was important that the family, tribe and clan did their best to gain this energy. As the individuals would either profit; gain reward - Meed, *Maed*(OE), or gather debt - Shild, *Scyld* (OE), in life by its effect. The stronger the Hamingja the stronger the self would be. Only the souls with the most Main could influence their after-death position (the spiritual realms of Valholl, Folkvang and Hel) or the circumstances of their rebirth back into the family, tribe and clan. Those souls with less main were at the mercy of their Orlog.

The way to gain positive Hamingja was to remain holy; to function as a part of the whole. This was done through conscious participation in all the sacred rituals that honoured the cycles of life/nature and to live by the ethical code of the clan. This wholeness was also developed within the self through meditation and the study and practise of runic knowledge and wisdom.

The practice of great deeds that tested the person's limitations, even unto death, also increased one's Speed and Main and contributed to individual and collective power and spiritual growth. The concept of Sin (*Synn*, OE) was any action or avoidance of action which took away power - speed and main - from the individual and/or the collective. This included non-honouring of the accepted ethical code of behaviour such as acts of cowardice.

When the supply of main had deteriorated, spiritual debt or obligation accumulated. This was called Skuld, *Scyld* (OE). Each skuld takes away from speed. Ethical deeds and acts of will to alter a difficult Wyrd such as bravery added to it. The ethical code of the Germanic heathens was based on values that encouraged the best from each individual.

These ethics have come to be collectively known, in the present, as the Nine Noble Virtues. These are Courage, Truth, Honor, Fidelity, Hospitality, Discipline, Industriousness, Self-Reliance and Perseverance.

In each lifetime, the state of the personal and collective Hamingja shows itself in your and your family's life circumstances, talents and opportunities. Below is a list of components that constitute the whole being - the psycho-somatic entity:

The Lyke (*Lìc*, OE) **is the body;** the vehicle through which we work our will and gain experience by the effects of its action.

The Hyde (*Hìd*, OE) **is the shape or form.** This is a more subtle energy than the Lyke but has its approximate shape. It contains all the energies of the psycho-somatic complex - the "skin of the soul". It carries the Ferth when faring forth in life and after death.

The High (*Hyge*, OE) **is the intellect** and includes analytical prowess and wilfulness. Its components are: The *Angit* (OE) - **the five senses** which collect information; The *Sefa* (OE) - **reason** and thought, the power of reckoning; The *Wit* (OE) - **memory** selection and retrieval.

The Mind (*Mynd*,OE) **is the cognitive consciousness.** Its component parts are: **The** *Myne* (OE) - **the personal reflective function**, memories, knowledge and wisdom; **The** *Orthanc* (OE) - **the source of ancestral memory** and instinct [Carl Jung's "CollectiveUnconscious"]. The Mind and the High work in close harmony. This is reflected on a bodily level as left and right brain functioning.

The Fetch (*Faecce*, OE and *Fylgja*, ON) **is a semi-independent being** attached to the soul during the lifetime of the body. It records all deeds of the 'souls' that have belonged to it. It is also seen as a warder or guardian. This entity is usually passed down the family line both to genetic and adopted members.

The Ferth (*Feorh*, OE) **is the soul-ghost** (*Gaest*, OE). It survives death of the body. It is the essence of the individual being; all the non-physical parts of the psycho-somatic complex that enter the spiritual realms.

The Wode (*Wòd*, OE) **is the seat of inspiration**. It is the source of extreme stimulation in forms ranging from madness to spiritual ecstasy. Harnessed by will, it can be used for great deeds of action and creativity. It is the divine seed of the self, similar to the Latin concept of *Genius*.

The Mood (*Mòd*, OE) **is the seat of all emotions** both simple and complex and is closely linked with the Wode, especially when expressed in noble feelings, such as honour and bravery.

The Will (*Willa*, OE) **is the force of self-determination**. It allows the harnessing of the thoughts from the Wode to be transformed into deeds. It can summon Wode (inspiration) and also Main (power) from hidden or runic (secret) places. It is part of the Ferth.

The Athem (*Aethem*, OE) **is the animating and unifying principle** that links the body with its non-material aspects. It holds the Ferth to the Lyke, the "cord" that binds body and soul during life and keeps connection while the Hyde is faring forth to other worlds. It is fed by the energies of food, drink and air during life but dissolves at the time of death, freeing the Ferth. If it does not dissolve entirely then the corpse remains animated and is known as a 'walking dead' (*Draugar*, ON). The Athem is also the medium for Main to be transferred to the Lyke.

Chapter Four
Time
and
Probability

There comes the maids   mighty in wisdom

Three from the sea That   beneath the tree stands.

Urdhr hight one   another Verdhandi

scored they on wood   Skuld is the third;

There they laws laid   There   they life chose

For men's children   and   orlog said.

(The Prophecy of the Seeress -
Poetic Edda. trans. by Eric Wodening)

50

Chapter Four
Time and Probability

The current view held by our Western Culture is that time is a linear projection of Past, Present and Future. The three concepts are seen as separate states that follow each other much as train carriages follow an engine past a static observation point. This triunal temporal concept and its consequent theory, that of absolute predestination, is a Judeo-Christian model and was accepted as doctrine by the medieval Church. St. Augustine (354-430 CE) formulated it in his books *The City of God* and *Confessions*.

This triunal premise sees time as a linear flow within a static universe which only exists in the mind of "God"; a universe that is fixed and closed. It gives forth the illusion that the past is unreachable and the future unchangeable. This concept is always oriented towards the future; that which is the present slips quickly into the past.

In contrast to this is the Germanic Heathen conception of time which is binary. In this model, the "future" does not exist. We still express this understanding in our language when we use the present tense to express the "future" as in phrases such as "Tonight we rest". Time consists of the past and the non-past which we call the present.

The past is the continually expanding container of all action from all beings who are existing and who have ever existed - "that which has been made manifest". The non-past is being continually drawn into the past as action manifests itself. With this concept, the past is continually shaping the non-past. It would be a mistake to view this as fatalism because without a concept of the future there can be no concept of a fixed fate.

In the Northern Tradition and non-separable from the nature of events - the concept of space, time and probability - are two main iconographic images; and a third concept which interweaves the two. These are the World Tree (called *Yggdrasil*, ON and/or *Irminsul*, OS), the Well of Wyrd (*Urdhr*, ON) and the Web of Wyrd. The word Wyrd is derived from *wurthi*, the feminine word for necessity.

The World Tree structures and contains the Multiverse (multiple dimensions). Again this differs from the Judeo-Christian concept of one reality (one God) - the Universe. The Well of Wyrd is the container of all events - it structures and contains time. The Web of Wyrd is the connecting force linking the two that reaches in all directions through out the Multiverse; a state of consciousness binding all realities, both actual and potential.

The World Tree stands above, with its roots in, the Well Of Wyrd. Besides the Well three giant beings nurture the Tree. They are collectively called the *Norns* (ME) and are also known as the "Wyrd Sisters". Their names in ON are **Urdhr - "That which has become"**, *Verdhandi* - **"That which is becoming"** and *Skuld* - **"That which shall (is obliged to) come"**. The word *urdhr* is the past participle of the verb *verdha*: that which has become, or turned. Verdhandi is the present tense of the same word; that which is turning. Skuld is derived from the verb *skulu* meaning shall, in this case that which shall be; debt or obligation.

The Norn called Urdhr (*Wurd*, OS and *Weird*, ME) controls the flow of events into the past and their influence out into the probability worlds of the non-past. Verdhandi governs the events that are in the process of happening - the immediate present. Skuld governs the actions that arise from necessity - the force of manifestation arising from the shaping power of all that has gone before. The collective duty of the Norns (*Nornir*, ON) is to "say the orlog" - lay down the primal layers

52

of events (which becomes the governing law) to ensure the unfolding of the Wyrd; the continuum of space, time and events in which the proper results of actions are manifested.

All actions do not have the same significance and so the Well of Wyrd is described as having three levels. Actions having a far reaching effect that impact on the flow of time settle into the deepest level. Those of lesser significance fall into the second level known as the Well of Mimir (mindfulness). Those of the least importance drop into the third level known as the Well of Hvergelmir (seething kettle). The World Tree (symbolic of all manifestation) draws its sustenance from the Well. The non-past (present actions) flowing into the Well become the past (that which has been layered down - Orlog) which in a returning flow (as determining factors) manifest the non-past (the present). The worlds of mankind and all supernatural beings are subject to the cosmic law of Orlog.

The Wyrd Sisters should not be confused with the Classical Fates of Greek tradition - *Clotho, Lachesis* and *Atropos* (although both variations derive from a common Indo-European source) who preordain the destiny of each individual - fix his fate. This Classical concept of time denies the ability to alter "that which is to come" and reduces the individual's life to that of an actor unconsciously enacting a pre-written script.

The Germanic Heathen concept of Time is an active state where events are unfolding as a result of what has happened and is happening now. To use the analogy of a Web further, one can envisage the "past" as threads of actions interwoven upon previous threads forming layers - a pattern. The "present" - "that which is becoming" is only a junction where these threads and layers join/overlap - the turning point. What we term the "future" - "that which shall come" is in reality only a potential weaving; a probability (not a reality) based on what is happening now and what has already happened.

Some patterns are of cosmic magnitude. Their origins and culmination are beyond our present awareness. Mankind has always sensed this with awe. Yet within these weavings we, as individuals, have the ability to alter the probabilities of the patterns yet un-manifested. By accepting responsibility for your own life, your actions and reactions, you give yourself the opportunity to change your Wyrd. Right action in the present accumulates personal power or Main (*Maegen*,OE) and luck or Speed (*Spaed*,OE). This conversion of action into potential positive energy enhances the exercise of your true will, accelerating your evolutionary path towards spiritual freedom.

Individuals who have developed their awareness of the patterns/layers can find themselves at any time poised - at the turning point - to take advantage of opportune circumstances. Time is a product of consciousness which is always in a state of flux.

By our present and past actions we put down layers of force into the Well that shape our lives - "that which shall become". By making a decision, we weave a thread into the Web that opens or closes another line of possible realities.

This concept of weaving time and events was recorded in the medieval Icelandic literary work of *Njàl's Saga* (1280 CE). As the story goes, just before the battle of Clontarf (Ireland 1014 CE), a man named Dorrud in the Viking settlement of Caithness (Scotland) saw twelve female riders disappear into a woman's bower. He approached the bower and looking through a window saw women standing before a loom which had men's heads for loom weights; men's intestines for the warp and weft; a sword for the beater and an arrow for the shuttle. They were chanting as they worked the loom.

Here is an extract from their chant:

Blood rains
From the cloudy web
On the broad loom
Of slaughter.
The web of man,
Grey as armour,
Is now being woven;
The Valkyries
Will cross it
With a crimson weft.

The warp is made
Of human entrails;
Human heads
Are used as weights;
The heddle-rods
Are blood-wet spears;
The shafts are iron bound,
And arrow are the shuttles.
With swords we will weave
This web of battle.

The Valkyries go weaving
With drawn swords,
Hild and Hjorthrimul,
Sanngrid and Svipul,
Spear will shatter,
Shields will splinter,
Swords will gnaw
Like wolves through armour.

(Translated by M. Magnusson & H. Palsson 1960)

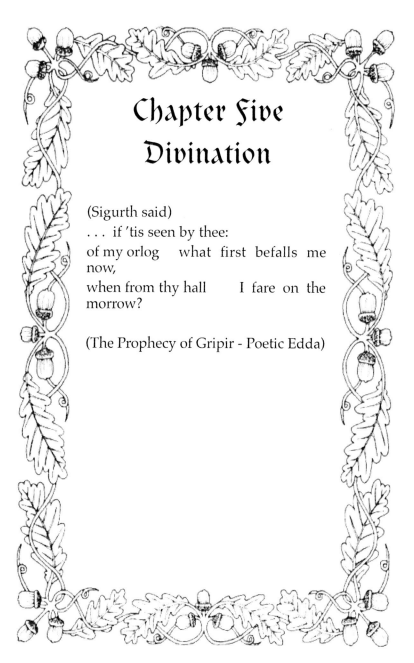

Chapter Five
Divination

(Sigurth said)
. . . if 'tis seen by thee:
of my orlog   what first befalls me now,
when from thy hall   I fare on the morrow?

(The Prophecy of Gripir - Poetic Edda)

Chapter Five
Divination

Divination: The act of divining, a prophecy, a prediction; inspired guesswork.

Divination is an esoteric art that is practised by cultures the world over. Reference to its many forms can be found throughout recorded history and beyond in the oral traditions.

It is generally categorised into two systems: Objective [analytical] and Subjective [inspirational]. To derive meaning, both types refer to symbols which provoke a verbal or visual response in the Diviner. These responses are synthesised with a previously-known reference and intuitional understanding.

The objective [analytical] system usually uses two main symbols which are superimposed to gain meaning. One symbol may refer to a category, the other may be an influence acting upon it.

Both sets of symbols have an external traditional reference. When they are melded an interpretation of their meaning is needed. This is done by applying knowledge with intuitional skill. Patterns of symbols are layed in a known manner to derive meaning.

Examples of this system are Astrological charts, Tarot card layouts and Celtic Ogham castings. The casting of runes belongs to this system.

In the subjective system, the diviner usually allows a portion of their conscious mind to receive information in a verbal or visual form from an inner or external source. The meanings are interpreted by the use of intuition, either by the diviner themselves or an aide.

Examples of this system are the direct forms of clairvoyance, clairaudience, psychometry and mediumship [currently called Channelling].

The objective system as exemplified by Rune casting uses both rational, intellectual knowledge and intuitional, inspired knowledge. This system uses both functions of the left and right brain. The subjective system uses direct experience of the inner and outer dimensions [sometimes referred to as the Unconscious Mind and/or the Superconscious] to gain hidden knowledge. This may or may not have a rational reference.

It is important to remember that objective and subjective divination sometimes overlap. Deep meditation on the analytical systems can trigger direct revelation and experience of altered states of consciousness. Subjective experience can lead to the tapping of hidden wisdom that is the backbone of the rational side of the analytical system. Both systems can be considered within the realms of Shamanistic practice.

The Runic methods of divination had their origins with direct experience and symbolic interpretation of their archetypal images. They enable the diviner to access realms of hidden knowledge reposited in the Collective Folk-Consciousness (*Minni*, OE). So the reading of the runes is a method to view the patterns of the Well/Web.

Our ancestors believed that the Gods and Goddesses spoke to humanity through the casting of the rune staves, giving advice and counsel, revealing that which is usually hidden from awareness. The runes give access to the actions and state of

Rune inscribed ankle bone of a Roe-deer used for divination, early 5th century. From a burial urn, England.

mind that has allowed the events to arise in the past to the present and that which may arise [as a result] in the future.

Consulting the runes can initiate the revelation of our "true" will - our deepest spiritual yearnings which are a source of power. Once we begin to know our spiritual potential, we can make a decision to change a pattern in our lives. Desire is not enough to alter events but it is the yeast that can catalyse thought into action. An understanding of the attitudes, actions and reactions that have put one in the present situation is needed.

The runes can allow the conscious mind to see what has been previously hidden from the self. If no change is sought, the runes will show the probable outcome. If change is sought, with an emphasis on understanding the underlying patterns -

61

the present, they will reveal the potential of the future that you can consciously manifest through your will. This is the Right Action to enact.

The divinatory function of the runes is not "fortune telling". It is the revelation of who you are now and what forces in nature, society and the inner self have shaped you to the present moment. What may come will be determined by your decision to act - every moment presents you with a turning point which will affect the Wyrd.

The heathen Germanic culture acknowledged that women especially had divination ability and were thus given great respect for their individual and tribal guidance. Those women among them who were consistent in their ability were called *Spækona* (ON) meaning a seeress, from *spae* - spy. The term *Vælva* (ON) was also given to those women with prophetic talents who also demonstrated other magical skills (witchcraft). Men who were practicing seers were called *Spæmadhr* (ON).

The priests (*Godhi*, ON) and priestess (*Gydhja*, ON) of the tribes, collectively called *Godhar* (ON) also took on divinatory functions when called upon especially in connection with gaining a deeper understanding of the patterns of the Wyrd that involved the interaction between humans and god/esses.

A Roman historian observed a Germanic Tribe enacting a divination rite in the First Century AD. It was recorded by Tacitus in his "Germania, 10":

"Their procedure in casting lots is always the same. They cut off a branch of a nut-bearing (ie. fruitful) tree and slice it into strips; these they mark with different signs and throw them completely at random onto a white cloth.

Then the priest of the state, if the consultation is a public one, or the father of the family if it is private, offers a prayer to the gods and looking up at the sky picks up three strips, one at a time, and reads their meaning from the signs previously scored on them.

If the lots forbid an enterprise, there is no deliberation that day on the matter in question. If they allow it, confirmation by the taking of auspices is required."

(Mattingly H. 1970 "Agricola and the Germania" Trans. S. A. Handford. Revised Harmondsworth.)

64

Chapter Six
The Runic Code

Knows't how to write,   knows't how to read

Knows't how to stain,   how to understand

Knows't how to ask,   knows't how to offer

Knows't how to supplicate, knows't how to sacrifice?

The Sayings of Har - Poetic Edda)

Chapter Six
The Runic Code

The first questions that prospective runers ask is "how do the runes work?", followed by "what can I do with them?".

The answer to the first question can not be simple in terms of material understanding as it traverses the fields of physics, psychology and para-psychology, what occultists collectively refer to as the theory of magick and what the followers of the Northern Tradition call the Primal [or Ur] Law. In the chapter (4) on Time and Probability the mechanics of orlog and wyrd were discussed and the chapter (5) on Divination explored the use of these frameworks for accessing knowledge. The chapter (3) on Soul Lore presents the heathen understanding of the psycho-somatic complex in relation to the Nine Worlds or Multiverse; and the chapter (13) on Magickal Applications of the Runes gives methods and uses for Rune Lore.

Throughout this book there are references to concepts such as the "Self", the "collective unconscious", "ancestral memory" and "racial memory". These are, of course, modern psychological terms but have been used to express an understanding of the Germanic Heathen's concepts of existence. Perhaps another model to act as a unifying theory would be appropriate at this stage. Dr. Rupert Sheldrake (1988.*The Presence of the Past: Morphic Resonance and the Habits of Nature*) has proposed the concept of organised fields of energy (such as referred to in association with the Rune Stave Uruz) that can act as blueprints for causality on a subtle level much like magnetic fields stimulate predictable responses to iron particles. He has named these organised energy patterns Morphic Fields and suggests that they all have a resonance which is named

Morphic Resonance. All structures down to an atomic level that have come into existence have a field and thus a resonance which is not dependent on space and time. Thus all structures, once coming into existence, can exert an influence on similar structures whether we designate them past, present or future; or with the runic terminology 'what is' and 'what should be'. In sympathetic magick, the saying is 'like attracts alike'. In terms of this theory, we would say that all fields exert a 'morphic resonance' that can be tuned into through the creation or the existence of a similar field - the Web of Wyrd.

Thus we can through the use of the rune staves tune into our ancestors and their society. We can explore former 'selves' - previous lives; the structure of life and its evolution; other worlds and states of being as well as other beings. We can explore the present and the potential of the future; gain wisdom and knowledge that no longer exists in material form. Through Morphic Resonance we can exert our influence on other 'organised fields', cause changes regardless of time and space; heal and hurt; improve or undermine the quality of life for others and ourselves - this is what we call magick and the runes are organised fields that exert resonance!

Freya's Aett: The awakening of the Self: The individual and collective social journey in the world - understanding Orlog - "That which has become".

ᚠ (Fehu):   Rune of Wealth and Status.

ᚢ (Uruz):   Rune of Strength and Tenacity.

ᚦ (Thurisaz):   Rune of Impulse and Reaction.

ᚨ (Ansuz):   Rune of Inspiration and Influence.

ᚱ (Raidho):   Rune of Advice and Action.

ᚲ (Kenaz):   Rune of Knowledge and Application.

X (Gebo):   Rune of Responsibilities and Obligations.

P (Wunjo):   Rune of Co-ordination and Contentment.

Hagal's Aett: The testing of the Self: The individual and collective psychological journey - experiencing Wyrd - "That which is becoming".

N (Hagalaz):   Rune of Adversity and Attitude.

| (Nauthiz):   Rune of Restrictions and Resources.

| (Isa):   Rune of Reduction and Reinforcement.

◊ (Jera):   Rune of Profit and Provision.

∫ (Eihwaz):   Rune of Endurance and Exploration.

[(Perthro):   Rune of Ritual and Revelation.

Y (Elhaz):   Rune of Defence and Assistance.

Ƨ (Sowilo):   Rune of Discrimination and
                           Determination.

Tyr's Aett: The actualising of the Self: The individual and collective spiritual journey - intuiting Skuld - "That which shall (is obliged to) come".

↑ (Tiwaz):   Rune of Law and Order.

ß (Berkano):   Rune of Feminine Function.

M (Ehwaz):   Rune of Instinct and Adjustment.

M (Mannaz):   Rune of Acceptance and Pragmatism.

Γ (Laguz):   Rune of Ferment and Fortitude.

◇ Ingwaz):   Rune of Masculine Fulfilment.

◇ (Othala):   Rune of Rights and Reclamation.

M (Dagaz):   Rune of Reconciliation and Realisation.

69

To be able to use the Runes for divinatory counselling, a basic understanding of their pattern is needed. The Futhark order, arranged in their Aetts, presents an evolution of consciousness.

Contemplate the runes, in order from Fehu to Othala, both as individuals and in their relationships to each other. Reverse this, going back from Othala to Fehu then contemplate the runes in pairs, from Fehu and Uruz to Dagaz and Othala (see Fig. 1).

Look at them within their groups of eight from Fehu to Wunjo, from Hagalaz to Sowilo, from Tiwaz to Othala; look at them also as pairs within a group and again as individuals in that group.

Now view them vertically in groups of three, taking a rune from corresponding positions in each eight, from Fehu, Hagalaz and Tiwaz through to Wunjo, Sowilo and Othala (see Fig. 3).

Look for numerological relationships, according to the Number Lore in this chapter. Use the same process to examine the detail of the relationships. This will help you to know the runes externally, strengthen your intuitive ability with them and gain an understanding of their evolutionary progression. The inner meaning of the runes will be revealed.

The application of number lore to the individual runes, studied separately, and in context to the Aetts, will reveal magickal possibilities to the astute runer.

I have chosen to use the alternative sequence for the last two runestaves as this order also appears in the Anglo-Saxon (and Anglo-Frisian) Futhorc (see Appendix) .

Freyja's Aett:

ᚠ	ᚢ	ᚦ	ᚨ	ᚱ	ᚲ	ᚷ	ᚹ
Fehu	Uruz	Thurisaz	Ansuz	Raidho	Kenaz	Gebo	Wunjo
1	2	3	4	5	6	7	8

Hagal's Aett:

ᚺ	ᚾ	ᛁ	ᛃ	ᛇ	ᛈ	ᛉ	ᛊ
Hagalaz	Nauthiz	Isa	Jera	Eihwaz	Perthro	Elhaz	Sowilo
9	10	11	12	13	14	15	16

Tyr's Aett:

ᛏ	ᛒ	ᛖ	ᛗ	ᛚ	ᛜ	ᛞ	ᛟ
Tiwaz	Berkano	Ehwaz	Mannaz	Laguz	Ingwaz	Dagaz	Othala
17	18	19	20	21	22	23	24

Record your observations for later reference.

As you complete these exercises, you may note the following patterns listed under the heading of Number Lore.

Also listed, for cross referencing, are charts of Colour Code, Elements, Correspondences and Traditional Rune Meanings to aid your study.

Number Lore

1   ᚠ   Origins, potentials, unified source.

1   ᚾ   Dynamic balance, dualities, cooperation, actualisation of potential. The doubling of qualities of number one.

3   ᚦ   Enclosed form, dynamic focussed energy.

4   ᚨ   Suspension, the controlled balance of opposing and harmonious forces. The mastery of material energy.

5   ᚱ   Human will in action. Self-expression within order.

6   ᚲ   The blending of dualities, integration, a doubling of the qualities of number three, life force, strength, divine motivation.

7   ᚷ   Conscious supernatural awareness, existential mysteries.

8   ᚹ   Unfolding material patterns, balance of energies, order and symmetry, resolution of action. A doubling of the qualities of number four.

9   ᚺ   Completion and the seed of new beginnings, the never-ending cycle, divine order through Cosmic Law. The sacred number of Rune Lore - nine being the compound of three times three.

10   ᚾ   New cycles based on old patterns, by the power of nine plus one. The results of human will in action, by the power of two times five.

11	|	Consolidation of individuality - I am, I will.
12	⟨	The perfection of materialisation, where spirit and matter vibrate in harmony. The power of four times three.
13	⟨	Development based on spiritual knowledge, the turning point of personal evolution. A new cycle, a compound of 12 plus one.
14	∫	Revelation of supernatural functions, mysteries explored. The qualities of two times seven.
15	Υ	The human will reaching for the numinous, through and beyond space and time. The qualities of five times three.
16	⟨	Utilisation of all resources to achieve harmonious existence, perfected power. The qualities of four times four and two times eight.
17	↑	Human will acting in balance with Cosmic Law.
18	ß	Potential contained, awaiting fruition; diversity from oneness. The qualities of two times nine and six times three.
19	⊓	Realisation of the essential unity of apparent opposites, sympathetic functioning. The compound of 18 plus one.
20	⋈	Self-mastery, perfected individual evolution based on an understanding of the Divine Structure within the human form. The power of four times five and two times 10.
21	Γ	Primal Energy, the supernatural source of all organic life. The power of seven times three and 20 plus one.

22	◇	Divine nourishment, the power of transmutation held in reserve. A compound of 18 plus four and 20 plus two.
23	◊	Self realisation and perfected function in the world. A compound of 20 plus three.
24	ᛗ	The Synthesis of spirit and matter resulting in transcendence, the Divine Paradox resolved. The power of six times four, eight times three and the compound of 20 plus four.

Colour Code

In the chapters on the 'Aettir' of the Elder Futhark - Freyja's Aett; Hagal's Aett; Tyr's Aett - there is given a colour correspondence to each rune stave and to each Hall of the god/ess associated. These are a combination of traditional lore and speculative association - intuition. The reader should meditate on these colour associations in the context that they are given within the chapters, especially when contemplating the Rune Rede of each stave. Additional colours of magickal importance are also given.

Light Blue: Motion and sensation - pervasiveness.

Dark Blue: Omnipresent mystical force - the numen.

Indigo: Manifested form - inertia before corrosion.

Purple: Corrosion - the force of dissipation.

Red: Stimulating force of vigour and magickal power but also of aggression/death.

Red-Gold: Universal power and honour; conversely
               tyranny and infamy.

Gold: Light of the Sun and the light of the spiritual
               realms.

Yellow: The will towards manifestation and material
               power.

Orange: Growth and fermentation towards new forms.

Orange-Red: Stimulating force of cosmic law underlying
               material manifestation.

Orange-Gold: Infusion of spiritual energy into manifested
               form.

White: Sum of all colours and the essence of purity and
               preservation.

Silver: Reflection and introspection - connecting force.

Dark Green: Organic life force striving for manifestation.

Green: The manifested organic life force of nature as
               fertility.

Rainbow: All potential in a state of flux - the spiritual and
               material matrix.

Black: The container of all light - contraction before
               expansion - imminent new beginnings.

The Elements

The Elements are forces of numinous reality that constitute the cosmos. These are:

Fire: Archetypal force of generation; primal expansive energy and magickal vibration; instinct/action; heat.

Air: Formlessness and movement; pervasiveness; light; thought/intellect; evaporation.

Water: Life Force and un-manifested form; magickal potential; evolutionary impetus; stillness; the unconscious mind - individual and collective; wetness.

Ice: Archetypal force of contraction; primal cohesive energy and non-vibration; coldness.

Earth: Organic manifestation and archetypal potential; structure and matter; existence; absorption.

Iron: Concentration of elements; reduction and transformation; synthesis; hardness.

Yeast: Catalytic organic structure; fermentative and trans-substantive; stimulative force of evolutionary change.

Salt: Inorganic manifestation; archetypal structure of matter; force of preservation; restructuring of form.

Venom: Primal energy of corrosion/dissolution; destructive and dissipative force of nature; necessary catalyst of transformation.

Chart of Correspondences

Colour	Tree	Herb	Element	Rune	God/ess	Animal
Red	Elder	Nettle	Fire	ᚠ	Freyja	Sow
White	Birch	Spagnum Moss	Salt	ᚾ	Vidar	Bull
Purple	Oak	House Leek	Venom	ᚦ	Thorr	Goat
Blue	Ash/Yew	Fly Agaric	Air	ᚨ	Odinn	Raven
Or-Red	Oak	Mugwort	Yeast	ᚱ	Jord	Cow
Red	Pine	Cowslip	Fire	ᚲ	Mani	Owl
Or-Gold	Ash/Elm	Heart-Ease	Yeast	ᚷ	Njord	Seal
White	Ash	Flax	Salt	ᚹ	Baldur	Stag
Indigo	Yew	Bryony	Iron	ᚺ	Hella	Dog
Purple	Beech/Rowan	Snake Root	Venom	ᚾ	Norns	Swan
Black	Alder	Henbane	Ice	ᛁ	Skadi	Reindeer
Green	Oak/Rowan	Rosemary	Earth	ᛃ	Sif	Vole
Red	Yew/Ash	Bryony	Fire	ᛇ	Ullur	Bear
Or-Red	Beech	Aconite	Yeast	ᛈ	Frigga	Falcon
Silver	Yew/Service	Sedge	Water	ᛉ	Heimdall	Ram
White	Juniper/Bay	Sage/Aconite	Salt	ᛋ	Sunna	Eagle
Indigo	Oak/Ash	Mistletoe	Iron	ᛏ	Tyr	Wolf
Green	Birch/Poplar	Lady's Mantle	Earth	ᛒ	Idunna	Beaver
Or-Gold	Ash/Elm	Ragwort	Yeast	ᛗ	Valkyries	Horse
Silver	Holy	Madder	Salt	ᛗ	Mimir	Hawk

Colour	Tree	Herb	Element	Rune	God/ess	Animal
Rainbow	Osier	Leek	Water	ᚱ	Ran	Sea Snake
Silver	Hazel	Self-Heal	Salt	◇	Ing-Freyr	Boar
Green	Hawthorn	Clover	Earth	⚸	Saga	Salmon
Indigo	Spruce	Clary	Iron	ᛗ	Forsetti	Stork

Traditional Rune Meanings

SHAPE	NAME	MEANING	SOUND	CONCEPT
ᚠ	Fehu	cattle, money	f	promordial fire / prosperity.
ᚢ	Uruz	aurochs	u	form / healing organisation.
ᚦ	Thurisaz	giant	th	r e s i s t a n c e / preconscsconscious.
ᚨ	Ansuz	a God (Odin)	a	inspiration/speech.
ᚱ	Raido	wagon	r	cycles/natural order.
<:ᚲ	Kenaz	torch	k, ch	regeneration/creativity.
ᚷ	Gebo	gift	g	exchange/binding.
ᚹ	Wunjo	joy	w, v	kinship/harmony.
ᚺ	Hagalaz	hail	h	transformation / crisis.
ᚾ	Nauthiz	need	n	need/constraint.
ᛁ	Isa	ice	i	concentration/self.

SHAPE	NAME	MEANING	SOUND	CONCEPT
ᚼ	Jera	year	j, y	harvest / renewal.
ᛁ	Eihwaz	yew	e / i	the World Tree/ initiation /death.
ᚲ	Perthro	dice-cup	p	chance/will/orlog.
ᛉ	Elhaz	elk	z	protection/ connection /wyrd.
ᛋ:ᛋ	Sowilo	sun	s	victory/success/ knowledge.
↑	Tiwaz	Tyr (the God)	t	courage/sacrifice / justice.
ᛒ	Berkano	birch	b	Birch Goddess/ rebirth /growth.
ᛖ	Ehwaz	horse	e	partnership/ shamanism.
ᛗ	Mannaz	human	m	primordial mankind/midgard.
ᛚ	Laguz	water	l	life energy/ emotion.
◇:ᛜ	Ingwaz	Ing (the God)	ng	gestation/fertility.
ᛞ	Dagaz	day	d	moment of being /enlightenment.
ᛟ	Othala	ancestral acres	o	inheritance / nobility / collective power.

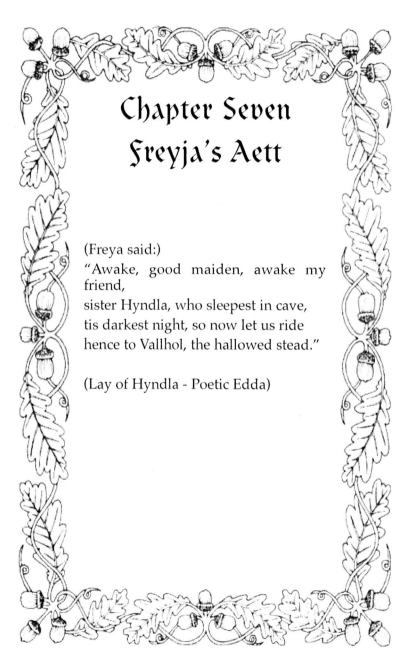

Chapter Seven
Freyja's Aett

(Freya said:)
"Awake, good maiden, awake my friend,
sister Hyndla, who sleepest in cave,
tis darkest night, so now let us ride
hence to Vallhol, the hallowed stead."

(Lay of Hyndla - Poetic Edda)

Rune 1

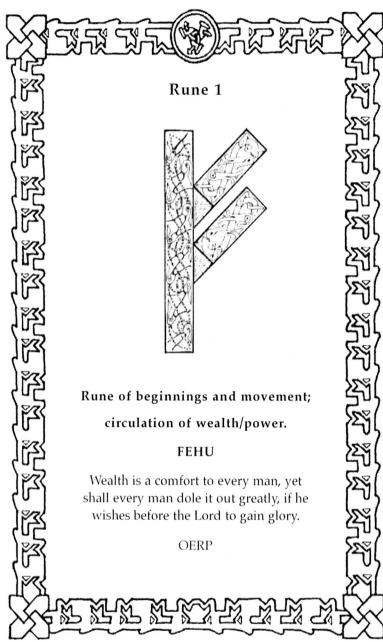

Rune of beginnings and movement;

circulation of wealth/power.

FEHU

Wealth is a comfort to every man, yet
shall every man dole it out greatly, if he
wishes before the Lord to gain glory.

OERP

ᚠ (Fehu): Rune of Wealth and Status.

Sound Value: f.   (pronounced "Fairh-oo")

Rune order sequence: No. 1.

Literal meaning: Cattle (mobile property - livestock, [generation of] money).

Esoteric meaning: Kinetic energy - the primal stimulating force of generation.

Magickal meaning: "Initiating Personal Power in Self and in the World".

Divinatory meaning: Prosperity.

Keywords: Stimulation; Beginning; Circulation of Power.

Colour: Red.   **Tree:** Elder.

Herb: Nettle.   **Element:** Fire.

Associated Deity: The Goddess Freyja - the "Lady".

The Goddess of love and war, riches and strife. She has first choice of slain warriors [an equal share goes to the god Odhinn, her masculine counterpart] and is the leader of the fierce feminine spirits known as Valkyries (choosers of the slain) who haunt the battle fields selecting worthy heroes to inhabit Valholl (hall of the slain/chosen) and Folkvang (field of the folk). She is also the goddess of ancestral feminine guardian spirits known as Disir. She is daughter of Njord/Jord (Nerthus), male/female deities of the Earth. She is twin to Freyr [masculine] and belongs to the category of God/esses of Nature and Fertility called Vanir. She is a Solar Goddess (Life Giver) as the Sun is feminine in Germanic Mythology.

She gained possession of the magical necklace called the Brisingamen (necklace of the Brisings, flaming necklace), made by four dwarfs, by having sex with each in turn. These four dwarfs were personifications of the four directions - North, South, East and West. The possession of the necklace gave her power over the earth-elements and associated spirits. It is said that she weeps tears of gold. Odhinn had the chaos-god Loki steal the Brisingamen for his self. Odhinn only returned it to Freyja when she caused war between two Kings that he wished to keep in alliance.

Her Hall is the home of courageous souls who have entered the ancestral realms but are attracted back into the world of Midgard (the Earth Realm). Her animal Fetch (familiar) is the Sow called Hildisvini (battle-swine).

Dwelling Hall: Folkvang - "Field of the Warrior-Folk".

Hall Colour: Light Blue. **Hall Symbol**: The Sow.

Hall Element: Earth. **Dominant Faculty:** Sensation.

Hall Matters: Personality, natural disposition, ethics, self-interest, personal power, worldly interest, wealth.

Need: Nurturing.

Attribute: Active. **Weakness:** Egotism.

Rune Rede for Fehu:

Shining Stave - Upright or Unobstructed:

New beginnings are imminent. Through increase of psychic drive, your will has been motivated. This is a period of active growth, erotic stimulation and the power of attraction that this state generates. An increase of status and/or prosperity are forthcoming. Expect more cultural activities and an expansion of esoteric knowledge/magickal force. Plan to use what you have gained for further increase. Share your wealth through the interest not the capital. This means nurture those who have supported you by providing a means for them to increase their own status. This may not be only financial but metaphysical as well. Demonstrate your love by practical means - you will gain respect. Your high ethical standard gain you respect within the community.

Shadow Stave - Reversed/Inverted or Obstructed:

You are not aware that any given moment can be a starting point for the rest of your life. Envy of other's possessions or influence undermines your integrity. Competitive greed or a hoarding consciousness is a selfish misuse of power. Conversly, moral lassitude can lead to atrophy of your present status, loss of support, loneliness and ultimately to a poverty of existence. Restriction of this rune energy disconnects you from the source of expansive impulse and, through involution, produces a "closed-circuit" structure of consciousness. Remember the myth of the gold-hoarding dragon Fafnir (embracer). He was overcome and slain by the magnanimous hero Sigurd who shared the spoils with his friends. Ambition is the motivation to action, and contentment is the result of grasping the moment. You will be measured more by your efforts than the results.

Fehu Key Words:

Shining Stave: Creation, beginnings, increase, movement, status, increase of prosperity, energy, power [will!], control, fertility, activation, growth. Psychic drive, motivation, erotic stimulation, esoteric knowledge, financial activities, animal culture, ambition, status, generosity, sharing.

Shadow Stave: Destruction, decrease, restriction, atrophy, lack of will power, broken spirit, lassitude, poverty, failure, loss, misuse of power, aggression, selfishness, hoarding.

Rune 2

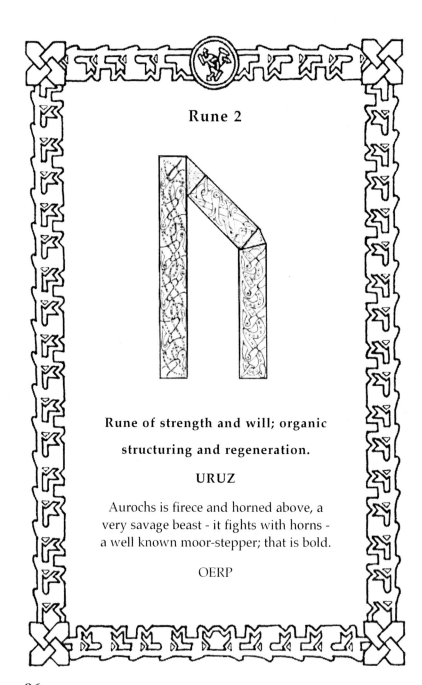

Rune of strength and will; organic

structuring and regeneration.

URUZ

Aurochs is firece and horned above, a
very savage beast - it fights with horns -
a well known moor-stepper; that is bold.

OERP

ᚢ (Uruz): Rune of Strength and Tenacity.

Sound Value: u. (pronounced "Oor-ooz")

Rune order sequence: No. 2.

Literal meaning: Aurochs (wild Oxen).

Esoteric meaning: Power of manifestation/regeneration; the power to protect same.

Magickal meaning: "Expanding and Protecting Self-Interest ".

Divinatory Meaning: Power and Agility.

Keywords: Primal Structure (causal); Organic Form.

Colour: White.   **Tree:** Birch.

Herb: Sphagnum Moss.   **Element:** Salt.

Associated Deity: The God Vìdar - "The Wide Provider".

He is known as 'The Silent', he is one of the Æsir [God/esses of Consciousness and Wisdom]. He is the strongest god after Thorr. Fathered by Odhinn, his mother Grid (greed) is of the Thurs (giant) race. He is the God of woodlands whose function is to maintain and protect the natural environment thus fulfiling the needs of those who live, and co-operate with each other, within Nature's Laws.

The great and fierce Aurochs (wild oxen) once inhabited the vast plains and woodlands of Europe. They could not be domesticated and could only be hunted to the death. The slaying of an Aurochs by a youth was often seen as his rite of passage to hunter/warrior. Warriors prized their horns which were used in ritual feasting as symbols of untamable [primal] vitality.

87

Vìdar's destiny is to avenge Odhinn at the time of Ragnarok (destruction of the powers) by tearing apart the jaws of the wolf Fenrir (fen-dweller), the devourer of his father, who has been raised in chains because of his ferocity. He will survive the final holocaust and return to the Idavoll plain (Place of Slendour) where the halls of the gods once stood.

His Hall is the source of the power of manifestation and preservation. His Fetch animal (familiar) is the Bull.

Dwelling Hall: Landvidi -   "Forest Land".

Hall Colour: Dark Green.   Hall Symbol: The Bull.

Hall Element: Earth.   **Dominant Faculty:** Sensation.

Hall Matters: Self-value, honour and fame, defense and aggression, possessions, gains and losses, health and stamina.

Need: Boundaries.

Attribute: Observing.   **Weakness:** Manipulative.

Rune Rede for Uruz:

Shining Stave - Upright or Unobstructed:

You have become aware of the life-force that permeates all structure. With this awareness comes the knowledge that mind and matter are interchangeable - consciousness determines the form of manifestation. This is an opportunity to recognise the "blue-print" of your own psycho-soul complex and thus re-form that which is not functioning in harmony with the whole, ie. self-healing. Know that the strength of your will continually creates and destroys the world of possibilities within the structure of your personal wyrd. This understanding generates courage, endurance and strength. Consciously plan to defend and fulfil your ideals. Healing and protective /nurturing ability with others is indicated. Good health and good luck are signified.

Shadow Stave - Reversed/Inverted or Obstructed:

Ignorance of the primal structure of reality can lead to avoidance of personal responsibility in health matters and fulfilment of your life's tasks. Learn to control your impulsive nature for self-preservation. Develop fortitude and don't be afraid to stand up for your beliefs but do not misuse your power to "bully" others who are weaker than yourself. Belligerence can lead to a "siege" mentality which can only result in an inability to help yourself, let alone others who would look to you for guidance. It's time you used your will and intellect to gain some depth of character - "grasp the bull by the horns"!

Uruz Key Words:

Shining Stave: Formation, patterns, vitality, strength, health, endurance, flexibility, foresight, understanding, wisdom, good fortune, reliability, courage, medical matters, nurturing, healing, protective force, possession, freedom.

Shadow Stave: Discord, decay, weakness, ill-health, lack of fortitude, rigidity, over-reaction, ignorance, perversity, cowardice, misuse of strength to control others for ego gain.

Rune 3

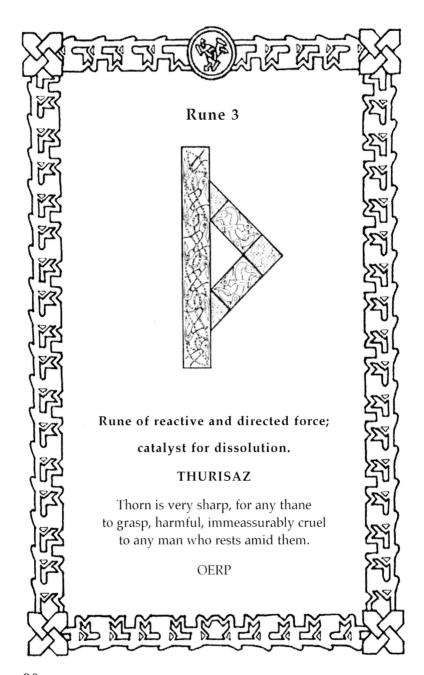

Rune of reactive and directed force;

catalyst for dissolution.

THURISAZ

Thorn is very sharp, for any thane
to grasp, harmful, immeassurably cruel
to any man who rests amid them.

OERP

þ (Thurisaz): Rune of Impulse and Reaction.

Sound Value: th.   (pronounced "Thoor-ees-arz")

Rune order sequence: No. 3.

Literal meaning: Giant, The Strong One, Thorn.

Esoteric meaning: Preconscious destructive forces of the natural world, external and internal.

Magickal meaning: "Resisting Degeneration and Dissolution".

Divinatory Meaning: Conflicts; Complexities.

Keywords: Corrosion; Aggression; Resistance.

Colour: Purple.   **Tree:** Oak.

Herb: House Leek.   **Element:** Venom

Associated Deity: The God Thorr - the "Giant".

He is called the Thunderer. Also known as Son of Earth. God of fertility and generation, Defender of the Realm of the Gods (Asgard) and the Mankind (Midgard), who together represent the Forces of Order, against the Thursar, primeval Forces of Natural Chaos personified as Giants. These beings are preconscious and instinctual beings/forces; a negative evolutionary factor necessary to dissolve form before reshaping can occur. Order and Chaos are both necessary for evolutionary momentum.

He uses his hammer, Mjollnir (lightning?) as his weapon in battle against the Giants but never involves himself in the battles of men. He is quick to anger but his solutions to problems show common sense and are swift and effective. He is

91

known as 'Deep-Thinker' because he outwitted the dwarf Alvis (All-wise) in a contest of magical knowledge. Son of Odhinn and Jord/Nerthus (Earth). Patron of all free men and those who work the Land. He shares qualities of both the Vanir [Nature and Fertility] and Æsir [God/esses of Consciousness and Wisdom].

His Hall is the place where the balance of instinct and reason is wrought. His animal Fetch (familiar) is the Goat.

Dwelling Hall: Thrudvang - "Field of Strength".

Hall Colour: Red.   **Hall Symbol:** The Goat.

Hall Element: Earth.   **Dominant Faculty:** Sensation.

Hall Matters: Hidden urges, unseen dangers, physical strength, environment, mental conflicts.

Need: Stability.

Attribute: Practicality.   **Weakness:** Anger.

Rune Rede for Thurisaz:

Shining Stave - Upright or Unobstructed:

Unconscious forces have been activated due to external stimulation. Through your awareness of the source, you can concentrate power and will, focus your energies to protect, defend and regenerate your situation. You are aware of the danger involved and will only use the force necessary to resist the pressure and resolve the conflict. You may be presented with an opportunity to break compulsive forms of behaviour that yourself or others no longer find supportive. These may be reactionary or just habitual but you know they are retarding your personal growth.

Shadow Stave - Reversed/Inverted or Obstructed:

You may feel you are in a chaotic situation where resistance to your thought, word or deed seems overwhelming. You may feel that you have lost control of the situation and perhaps self-control. It is important that you don't over react at this present time nor lapse into neurotic or sociopathic behaviour. Nor should you tolerate it from others. You are not defenceless. Transmute your fear/anger into a single minded determination to overcome the cause of the problem. Allow outside help if necessary.

Thurisaz Key Words:

Shining Stave: Concentrated power and will, applied force, reaction through stimulation, needed action, brute strength, male potency, eroticism, righteous conflict, defence, regeneration, protector, awareness of danger, petty annoyances.

Shadow Stave: Chaos, corrosion, dissolution, destruction, brutality, misdirected force, stupidity, obsession, peril, betrayal, psychological problems, sexual compulsion, enemies, crisis, sociopathic behaviour, defencelessness.

Rune 4

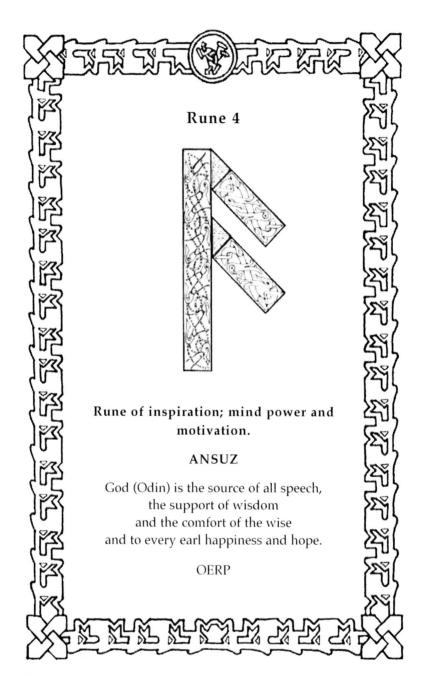

Rune of inspiration; mind power and motivation.

ANSUZ

God (Odin) is the source of all speech,
the support of wisdom
and the comfort of the wise
and to every earl happiness and hope.

OERP

ᚨ (Ansuz): Rune of Inspiration and Influence.

Sound Value: a. (pronounced "Arns-ooz")

Rune order sequence: No. 4.

Literal meaning: Ancestral God, Odhinn, Mouth.

Esoteric meaning: The God/esses as the all pervasive source of consciousness.

Magickal meaning: "Agitation of Mind and Mood".

Divinatory Meaning: Spiritual Blessings.

Keywords: Archetypal Source; Light/Sound Vibration.

Colour: Blue.   **Tree:** Ash/Yew.

Herb: Fly Agaric.   **Element:** Air.

Associated Deity: The God Odhinn - "Frenzy", the "Inspirer".

The God of magick, secret wisdom and death. He receives half of the slain warriors [Freyja, the other half]. The archetypical magician, shape-shifter and shaman - giver of the Runes. He is also the god of poetry and intellectual insight. He can inspire either enlightenment or madness. In his original function of Psychopomp (guide to souls of the dead) he rides an eight-legged horse named Sleipnir (slipper). Over time, he became the leader of the Gods - the "All-father". He is the god of wisdom gained through knowledge and experience.

He travels amongst the living and the dead as Gangleri (wanderer) disguised as an old man with a staff, garbed in a hooded cloak or with a slouch hat pulled over his empty eye socket. He gave one of his eyes as a sacrifice to the Well of Mimir (mindfulness) in exchange for ancient knowledge. This search for wisdom and knowledge is said to be for the purpose of ascertaining the circumstances leading up to, and for the holding back of, the onset of the final battle between Order and Chaos known as Ragnarok (destruction of the powers).

He is a complex and contradictory character whose motivations one can never be sure of. From his High Seat Hlidskjalf (gate-tower?), he sees all happenings, and hears all from his two ravens - Huginn (thought) and Muninn (memory) - who travel throughout the "Nine Worlds" (the nine dimensions of the Universe of which he and Mankind have access). His throne is protected by the twin wolves Geri (greed) and Freki (rapaciousness).

His Hall is the matrix of integrated consciousness. His animal Fetch (familiar) is the Raven.

Dwelling Hall: Gladsheim - "Home of Gladness".

Hall Colour: Dark Blue.   **Hall Symbol:** The Raven.

Hall Element: Air.   Dominant Faculty: Thought.

Hall Matters: Information technology, facts, education, studies, writings, mental inclinations and abilities, short journeys.

Need: Individuality.

Attribute: Daring.   **Weakness:** Stubborn.

Rune Rede for Ansuz:

Shining Stave - Upright or Unobstructed:

Inspirational excitation is coming to you from the highest sources - the plane of Divine Consciousness. Use your intellectual abilities to synthesise this energy into a form that stimulates change in your life. Arcane wisdom permeates all aspects of your comprehension and abilities. You now have the ability and maturity to communicate and/or manipulate this wisdom, and influence others to seek the same. The power surging through you peaks in ecstatic and emotive mind states. This upliftment can be expressed through poetry, prose, art, music, science and mathematics. Recognition of symbolic meaning allows magickal focus which can be expressed through divination, visualisation and Galdar (singing, chanting, writing) magick with the runes, and other power symbols. Enhance your culture with your gifts but be aware that you may be looked on by others with suspicion and mistrust.

Shadow Stave - Reversed/Inverted or Obstructed:

Ignoring intuitive inspiration can result in poor judgement, befuddled thoughts and the inability to express yourself adequately. Dullness of intellect breeds delusion and leaves you wide open to manipulation by others through oratory, hypnosis and psychic attack. A sense of discontent pervades all your efforts at learning new skills and technology may scare you. This breeds a tendency for pretence of knowledge and/or wisdom. You may think you are fooling others by your arguments and sophistry but really you are only fooling yourself. Measure your imagination on the scales of accumulated ancestral knowledge/wisdom. Is there any validity to your fear/fancy? Beware of becoming lost in obsessive thoughts, emotions and/or prejudice - this is the "Freeway" to madness. Start meditation and methodical study in your areas of interest. Your focus is too narrow. Develop an open mind and hone your power of discrimination.

Ansuz Key Words:

Shining Stave:　　Inspiration from divine source, cognition, comprehension, transformation, psychic abilities, mastery of words and language, creative use of same, communication, use of acquired knowledge and experience, spiritual wisdom, intellect, ecstasy, order, synthesis, hypnotic ability, power of persuasion.

Shadow Stave: Dullness, misunderstanding, delusion, psychic attack, madness, confusion, poor judgement, inability to communicate, manipulation by others, discontent, ignoring intuition.

Rune 5

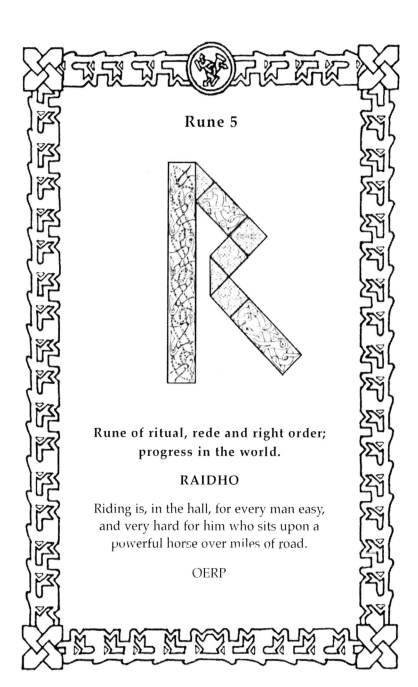

**Rune of ritual, rede and right order;
progress in the world.**

RAIDHO

Riding is, in the hall, for every man easy,
and very hard for him who sits upon a
powerful horse over miles of road.

OERP

ᚱ (Raidho): Rune of Advice and Action.

Sound Value: r.   (pronounced "Raydh-oh")

Rune order sequence: No. 5.

Literal meaning: Riding (out), Chariot, Wagon.

Esoteric meaning: Controlled progress through 'tried and true' activity.

Magickal meaning: "Extending Control through Right Action".

Divinatory Meaning: Correct Judgement.

Keywords: Counsel; Re-enforcement; Ritual.

Colour: Orange-Red.   **Tree:** Oak.

Herb: Mugwort.   **Element:** Yeast

Associated Deity: The Goddess Jord - "Earth".

Also known as Fjorgvin her name is cognate with 'earth' and 'land'. She is the Nerthus (Mother Earth) worshipped by the Germanic tribes of the North Sea region. She is the twin of Njord, the parents of the twin deities Freyr and Freyja and the mother of Thorr by a union with Odhinn. Her mother was said to be Nott (night).

Her worship included the procession of a wagon throughout the countryside every springtime to give the blessing of fecundity to the land, animals and humans. During this time, all weapons were laid aside and the people gave themselves over to feasting and love making. Votive rites were performed in the fields and forests to remind the folk of the cyclic nature of life. No one was allowed to look upon the Earth Mother's image except for her male priests and two attendants who were chosen anew every year. At the end of the tour the wagon

100

and image were returned to a sacred island. The servants of the goddess bathed and redressed the image. They were then ritually sacrificed, by strangulation and drowning, in a spring sacred to the goddess.

Her Hall is home of Natural Order. Her animal Fetch (familiar) is the Cow.

Dwelling Hall: Lyfjaberg -   "Hill of Living".

Hall Colour: White.   Hall Symbol: The Cow.

Hall Element: Earth.   **Dominant Faculty:** Sensation.

Hall Matters: Life cycles and harmony, fertility, adaption, travel, healing, litigation, counseling, personal rights.

Need: Nurturing.

Attribute: Perseverence.   **Weakness:** Procrastination.

Rune Rede for Raidho:

Shining Stave - Upright or Unobstructed:

You are prepared to test your theories, put your plans into action. By measuring your progress, ie. planning your activities for the best timing and preparing to repeat those that gain results, you will create a harmony that attracts fortuitous circumstances - luck. Listen to advice from traditional or experienced sources, those who have undertaken long term goals and succeeded, and you will find the right path. Your journeys whether internal of external will be successful if you allow natural cycles to determine periods of pause and action. It is important that your attention does not waver too far from the goals set by yourself, for yourself.

Shadow Stave - Reversed/Inverted or Obstructed:

If dealing with the external world, your values and prejudices will be challenged. If your movement is mystical/spiritual/religious, then your desire for security will be confronted. You cannot attain maturity by avoiding change nor by running away from challenges by pretending to yourself, and to others, that they are of no consequence. You can block your own opportunities by feeling victimised. Reflect on your daily life and ask yourself if you may have taken the "wrong path". Stop sulking, it's time to "walk your talk".

Raidho Key Words:

Shining Stave: Harmonic action, right timing, ritual activity, preparedness, ordered movement, travel, the right path, spiritual growth, religion, advice based on truth, right judgement, a quest, tradition, evolutionary activity, experience, legal actions.

Shadow Stave: Irrational activity, poor perception of cause and effect, crucial moment, blocked opportunities, strain, stasis, daily grind, injustice, wrong direction, forced relocation, spiritual crisis.

Rune 6

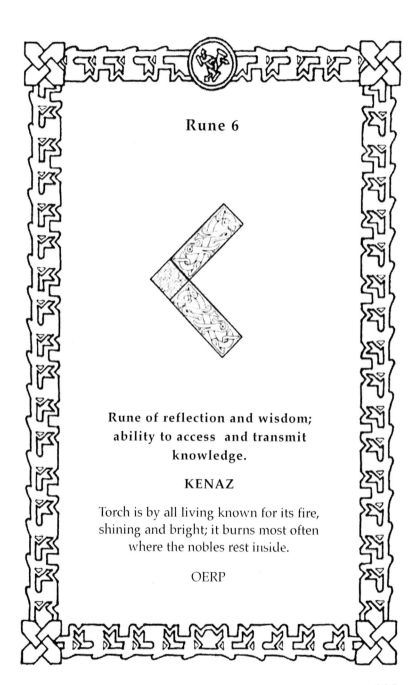

**Rune of reflection and wisdom;
ability to access and transmit
knowledge.**

KENAZ

Torch is by all living known for its fire,
shining and bright; it burns most often
where the nobles rest inside.

OERP

ᚲ (Kenaz): Rune of Knowledge and Application.

Sound Value: k. (pronounced "Kairn-arz")

Rune order sequence: No. 6.

Literal meaning: Torch (illumination), Cremation Fire.

Esoteric meaning: The "fire" of intellect, consciousness and creative skill.

Magickal meaning: "Recognition of Connective Relationships".

Divinatory meaning: Transmission of Collective Knowledge.

Keywords: Intensity; Focus; Transformation.

Colour: Red.   **Tree:** Pine.

Herb: Cowslip.   **Element:** Fire.

Associated Deity: The God Mani (the "Man-in-the-Moon").

He is the moon personified, the son of Mundilfari (turner?). His job is to drive the chariot carrying the physical moon across the night sky. He is the brother of the goddess Sunna (also known as Sol by the Vikings) who personifies the Sun and who is the charioteer of that heavenly body. Sunna is said to be the manifested (material) eye of Odhinn, just as her brother Mani represents Odhinn's other (spiritual) eye which he sacrified into Mimir's (mindfulness) Well for the gaining of wisdom.

His function is to govern the waxing and waning of the moon by his orbital passage and thus exert his influence on the rhythms of nature in the sea, the land and the human body. He also acts as an illuminator of consciousness through reflecting the light of Sunna's charge to stimulate the hidden tides of thought and memory during the quiet of the night. He drives a wagon drawn by a horse called Hrimfaxi (ice-mane) and is pursued by a wolf-shaped troll called Hati (destroyer) from the place called Jarnvidr (iron wood) in Jotunheim (home of the giants). Hati will devour him at Ragnarok (destruction of the powers) which is the final battle between the forces of order and chaos.

His hall is the home of learning and teaching. His animal Fetch (familiar) is the Night-Owl.

Dwelling Hall: Velsofa -   "Sleep Ease".

Hall Colour: Silver.   **Hall Symbol:** The Night-Owl.

Hall Element: Water.   **Dominant Faculty:** Intuition.

Hall Matters: Hereditary talents, racial memories, creativity, sexuality, biorhythms, illness.

Need: Serenity.

Attribute: Adaptive.   **Weakness:** Vacillating.

Rune Rede for Kenaz:

Shining Stave - Upright or Unobstructed:

Creative focus arises when tension is minimal. Your inclination for quiet reflection allows you to see the possibilities of potential transformation of the subject/object of contemplation. Concentration with intent can shape your desires into goals what will eventually become reality. Your abilities may revolve around artistic, technical, academic and/or magickal skills. The vital force of life is constantly seeking to generate form. Creative power in any field of expression is intrinsically interwoven with sexuality. Joyous and passionate encounters/ relationships are indicated. The enjoyment of, or the desire for, off-spring is present. You can now create new opportunities for yourself/family by using your talents. You may find the opportunity to pass on your accumulated knowledge to the benefit of all concerned.

Shadow Stave - Reversed/Inverted or Obstructed:

Your present lack of creativity is causing festering emotions which spoil your appreciation of life. If you continually focus on stressful thoughts and/or situations your blockage will have long term, and possibly serious, effects on your health. It will also further decrease your vital energy resulting in decreased sexual interest, and naturally affect your erotic personal relationships. A lowering of self-esteem follows, and a further increase of stress results. Family and work relationships will suffer. Take time out to relax, meditate and/or contemplate. The neglecting of your skills/talents shows an inability to give your personal interests equal priority with other demands/needs in life. Put time aside for hobbies, sports, special interests. Spend more time on yourself. It is not selfish, it is essential for your flow of creativity. Your sex life will be better too! Observe the joyous concentration of children in play. Seek out the company of those who practise their skills rather than theorise. Make an attempt to learn from these cunning ones.

Kenaz Key Words:

Shining Stave: Use of creative potential, artistic, technical and teaching ability, craftsmanship, controlled energy, knowledge, insight, teaching, transformation, regeneration, sexual energy, joyous passion and lust, transfiguration, revitalisation, healing, new directions, opportunities, children [offspring], personal relationships.

Shadow Stave: Lack of creativity, non-use of skills, degeneration, disease, aggravation of existing illness, breakdown, consumation by negative emotions, inability to learn from experience.

106

Rune 7

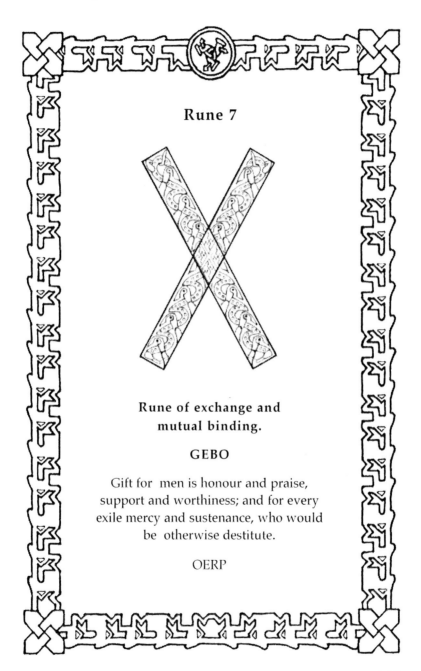

**Rune of exchange and
mutual binding.**

GEBO

Gift for men is honour and praise,
support and worthiness; and for every
exile mercy and sustenance, who would
be otherwise destitute.

OERP

ᚷ (Gebo): Rune of Responsibilities and Obligations.

Sound Value: g. (pronounced "Gairb-oh")

Rune order sequence: No. 7.

Literal meaning: Gift, Giving.

Esoteric meaning: Exchange of energy between spirit and matter.

Magickal meaning: "Binding of Individuals into Mutual Dependence".

Divinatory Meaning: Generosity and Hospitality.

Keywords: Polar attraction; Exchange.

Colour: Orange-Gold.   **Tree:** Ash/Elm.

Herb: Heartease.   **Element:** Yeast

Associated Deity: The God Njord - The "Earth Enjoyer".

He is known as the 'Blameless ruler of all men'. God of the sea-shore, water-ways, ships/cargo and all associated wealth. Patron of all those whose livelihood comes by or from the water-ways and sea. Patron god of all riches. Known as a reconciler. Consort/brother to Jord/Nerthus (the Earth Goddess). Father to Freyr/Freyja. He is one of the Vanir who was left as a hostage with the Æsir at the end of the great war between these god-races.

Short-time husband to Skadi (harm), Warrior Goddess of the Mountains who selected him as her husband in compensation for her father Thjazi (self-serving) who was slain by Thorr. The choice was made on viewing his beautiful feet - she was not allowed to see his whole body. She mistook him for the god

Baldur (bold), son of Odhinn and Frigga. They separated after sharing nine days together in each others realms.

His Hall is the home of worldly gain and its management. His Fetch (familiar) animal is the Seal.

Dwelling Hall: Noatun -   "Harbour".

Hall Colour: Gold.   **Hall Symbol:** The Seal.

Hall Element: Water.   **Dominant Faculty:** Intuition.

Hall Matters: Religious practice, self-value, extended family, domestic affairs, contracts, property.

Need: Friendship.

Attribute: Private.   **Weakness:** Non-appreciation.

Rune Rede for Gebo:

Shining Stave - Upright or Unobstructed:

Gifts are a circulation of energy and a form of binding. You may be the recipient or the giver, according to your position. Exchange may be on equal terms such as contracts, personal relationships or contact with spiritual/magickal forces such as personal deities, or spirit guides/guardians. Expect loyalty and favourable emotive sharing as there is understanding of mutual interdependence. Celebration and hospitality are favoured. Generosity will be rewarded and as such as it is in all exchanges, both parties must trust that the other will honour both the form and intention of the gift. A favourable time for pledged commitment and marriage.

Shadow Stave - Reversed/Inverted or Obstructed:

If you find yourself losing favor from higher authorities (spiritual or temporal), friends or loved ones, review your sensitivity. Are you depressed of lonely? Do not try to buy influence or favor, nor let yourself be manipulated by greed for your own or others' purposes. Generosity is pure only when it is enacted from love or compassion. Other forms of giving are really contracts for mutual gain but are not wrong in themselves if you recognise their nature and accept the conditions. If you are feeling subservient, then it is time to review your current relationships, either personal or communal. A choice may have to be made between freedom and responsibility.

Gebo Key Words:

Shining Stave: Binding force, oaths, partnerships, gifts, generosity, loving exchange, magickal force, personal relationship, contracts, sexual union, marriage, charities, hospitalities, feasts.

Shadow Stave: Manipulation, subserviance, greed, loss, depression, loneliness, generosity detrimental to self (buying status), loss of favour from higher authority, spiritual or temporal.

Rune 8

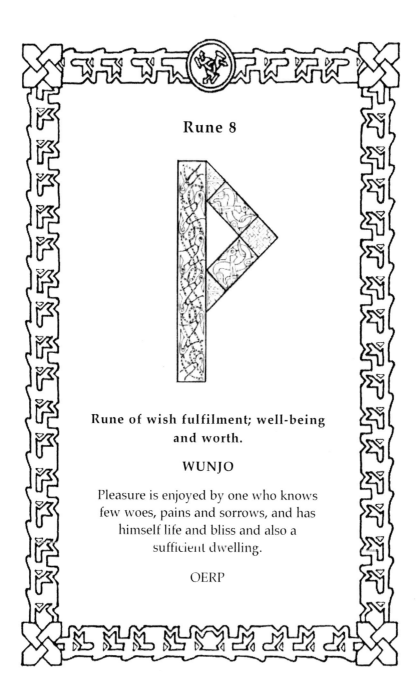

**Rune of wish fulfilment; well-being
and worth.**

WUNJO

Pleasure is enjoyed by one who knows
few woes, pains and sorrows, and has
himself life and bliss and also a
sufficient dwelling.

OERP

ᛩ (Wunjo): Rune of Coordination and Contentment.

Sound Value: w.   (pronounced "Voon-yoh")

Rune order sequence: No. 8.

Literal meaning: Pleasure; Winning; Peace (absence of woe).

Esoteric meaning: Perfection; Magickal will; Wish fulfilment, Clan mental bonding.

Magickal meaning: "Using the Collective to gain Individual Fulfilment".

Divinatory Meaning: Joyful Recognition of Worth.

Keywords: Contentment; Fellowship.

Colour: White.   **Tree:** Ash.

Herb: Flax.   **Element:** Salt.

Associated Diety: The God Baldur - the "Bold".

The God of youth, hope and courage but with the peculiarity that his decisions had no effect in the realm of the gods. He embodies the hidden seed of the new world to come after the end of this world cycle. Son of Odhinn and his wife Frigga (lady), Goddess of silent wisdom and duty, husband of Nanna (mamma?). One of the Æsir, he will inherit his father's throne as chief of the gods.

Having premonitions of his death, Frigga asked all things not to harm Baldur, except for the Mistletoe which she considered "too young" and thus harmless. The Mistletoe was fashioned into a spear by Loki (the trickster-god) and while the gods were having sport by casting weapons at Baldur, the blind-god Hodur (warrior) was given the mistletoe spear which he cast and killed Baldur. Nanna joined him in Hel (concealed) - the place of the dead - by throwing herself on his funeral pyre. Odhinn tried to ransom Baldur from Hel - the acceded condition given was that all things weep for Baldur's death. Through Frigga's pleas, all things did weep except for Loki. So Baldur awaits his rebirth in Hel - from where he sends presents to Frigga - until after Ragnarok (destruction of the powers).

His Hall is place of the realisation of the true will. His animal Fetch (familiar) is the Stag.

Dwelling Hall: Breidablik - "Broad Shining".

Hall Colour: Yellow.   **Hall Symbol:** The Stag.

Hall Element: Fire.   **Dominant Faculty:** Feeling.

Hall Matters: Associations, desire to affect the world, spiritual awakening, arts, leisure, pleasure, romance, children.

Need: Admiration.

Attribute: Honourable.   **Weakness:** Attachment.

Rune Rede for Wunjo:

Shining Stave - Upright or Unobstructed:

A trouble free time can be expected. You are at peace with yourself, so relax and enjoy yourself. Seek out the company of like-minded people. "Club" activities are stimulating and rewarding. This is a time of domestic and social tranquillity, also a time of prosperity, so business relationships may prove rewarding with good prospects for expansion. Your accomplishments attract attention. Celebrate your good fortune with friends and family. For some, the purchase or paying off of their ideal home and/or property. For others it means delight in retirement from the hard work at hand with goals attained and feeling contented. For those of a spiritual/religious nature there is a euphoric sense of bonding with the higher self

113

and/or with your spiritual peers/siblings or congregation - you know you are not alone.

Shadow Stave - Reversed/Inverted or Obstructed:

You are feeling alienated from self and society. Unfulfilled expectations are permeating you with a sense of loss and sadness. Setbacks and strife in your family, work place or special interest group have left you with a yearning for recognition, of worth. Be careful not to lose your identity by merging with the "group consciousness", nor should you try to dominate to get your own way. Re-examine your approach to others in attaining your heart-felt desires. Make friends with yourself first then you can begin to seek out your true will. Maybe you need to change your job or associates, maybe just your attitude! Find those who appreciate and share your aspirations. This makes possible the bearing of life's trials with good humour.

Wunjo Key Words:

Shining Stave: Reward, wish fulfillment, gain, accomplishment, celebration, prosperity, harmony of like elements, fellowship and joy, contentment, domestic tranquility, social relationships/services and material prosperity, coping ability.

Shadow Stave: Unfulfilled expectations, loss, retardation, setbacks, sadness, strife, alienation from spiritual world, family and/or common interest groups.

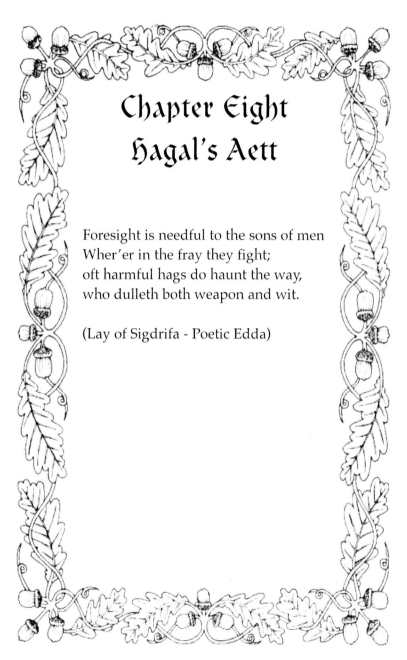

Chapter Eight
Hagal's Aett

Foresight is needful to the sons of men
Wher'er in the fray they fight;
oft harmful hags do haunt the way,
who dulleth both weapon and wit.

(Lay of Sigdrifa - Poetic Edda)

Rune 9

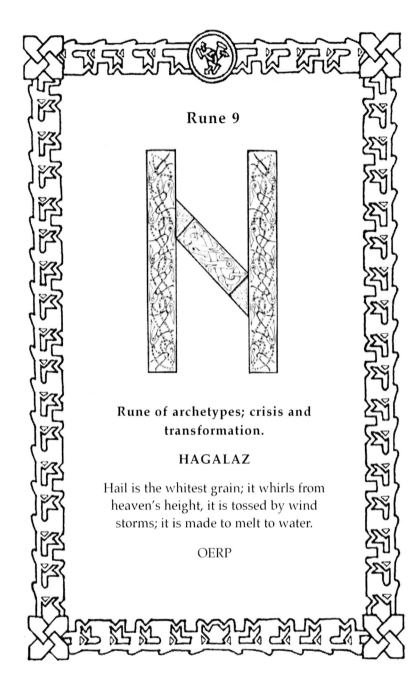

**Rune of archetypes; crisis and
transformation.**

HAGALAZ

Hail is the whitest grain; it whirls from
heaven's height, it is tossed by wind
storms; it is made to melt to water.

OERP

ᚺ (ᚺagalaz): Rune of Adversity and Attitude.

Sound Value: h.   (pronounced "Harg-arl-arz")

Rune order sequence: No. 9.

Literal meaning: Hail, Spear-attack.

Esoteric meaning: The synthetic seed of all potential manifestation.

Magickal meaning: "Utilising Disruption for Self-Evaluation".

Divinatory Meaning: Uncontrolled Forces; the Orlog.

Keywords: Crisis; Transformation.

Colour: Indigo.   **Tree:** Yew.

Herb: Bryony.   **Element:** Iron

Associated Diety: The Goddess Hella - the "Concealer".

She is Ruler of the realm of the dead specifically those who perish from illness or old age. Her realm called Hel (concealed) is within Niflheim (misty home) and is dark and quiet, the resting place of all souls awaiting rebirth, and with them all their life knowledge, memories and dreams. It is said to be nine days 'ride' from Midgard (realm of the living). A deeper hall called Nàstrandir (shore of corpses) was reserved for evil doers who passed through Hel to die a second death by the dragon called Nidhogg (vicious blow) who also chews on the roots of the World Tree (Yggdrasil).

Hella's appearance is frightening as one side of her is a rotting corpse and the other is beautiful. She eats of a plate called Hunger with a knife called Famine. She is the daughter of the

117

giantess Angrboda (distress bidder) by Loki (Odhinn's "blood-brother" who has the ability to change sex and/or be hermaphroditic). She is the sister of the wolf Fenrir ('fen dweller) who devours Odhinn at Ragnarok (destruction of the powers) and the Midgard-Serpent Jormungand (mighty wand) who encircles the earth biting his own tail. As a psychopomp, she is the feminine counterpart of Odhinn, being a knowledge-guardian and protector of souls awaiting rebirth.

Her hall shelters the mysteries of life and death and can only be approached through the the entrance named Nàgrind (corpse gate). Her animal Fetch (familiar) is guardian of Nàgrind, the Hound-Dog called Garm (rag).

Dwelling Hall: Elvidnir -   "Misery".

Hall Colour: Black/ White.   **Hall Symbol:** The Dog.

Hall Element: Earth.   **Dominant Faculty:** Sensation.

Hall Matters: Environmental stress, natural calamities, enemies, unlearnt lessons, parents, sickness, death.

Need: Insight.

Attribute: Steadfast.   **Weakness:** Pettiness.

Rune Rede for Hagalaz:

Shining Stave - Upright or Unobstructed:

Through crisis you have realised that your way of dealing with yourself, others and situations has ceased to be viable. Now is the time to seek new archetypal models within yourself, from which you may derive impetus. Through finding harmony within you can take control and turn seeming disaster into success. Hagalaz is called "the Mother Rune" as it contains all the potential of the other runes - it is the seed of all possibilities. So take advantage of this cycles end, accept what has occurred or is occurring. Design a new approach that will

118

transform what appears to be misfortune into the structure for you, to not only survive and thrive, but to help others do the same. Through this acceptance you will learn to use all crisis as a chance to discover your own and others deepest strengths/weaknesses. Make use of this knowledge by leaving others with the feeling that their world is a better place for having known you.

Shadow Stave - Reversed/Inverted or Obstructed:

Drawing this rune is a warning. Traumatic circumstances are manifesting. You are being confronted by your wyrd (the sum expression of your thoughts and deeds up to the present). You may feel that situations are beyond your control, either from natural causes or from overwhelming circumstance. Do not try to avoid the situation or its aftermath. Find the quiet "eye of the cyclone". Rather than react, take careful stock of your choices, then choose a path of action. Observe the world of nature - new growth always follows destruction. In humans, new growth can only occur if they let the critical experience stimulate them to change their attitudes - whether these are to do with others beliefs/ methods or your own. Do not abandon your goals but find a more appropriate platform to achieve them. If you remain defensive or resistant, you face loss of power and ruin.

Hagalaz Key Words:

Shining Stave: Change within an evolutionary frame-work, lessons learnt, seed of all potential, controlled critical situations, completion according to a plan, internal harmonisation, mysticism.

Shadow Stave: Natural disruptions, situations beyond control, abandonment of goals, catastrophe, loss of power, unlearnt lessons, financial ruin, disaster, stagnation.

Rune 10

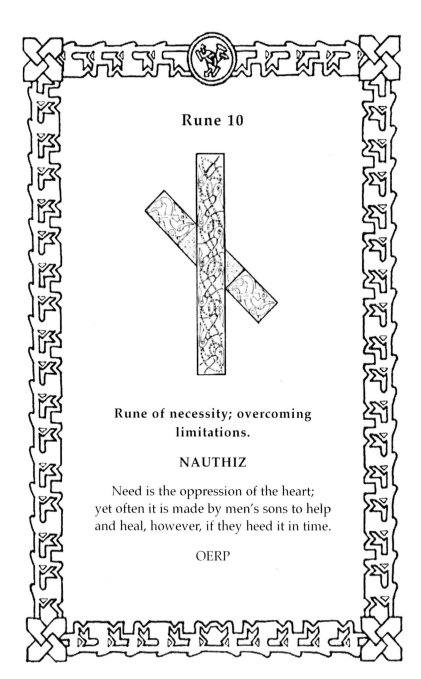

**Rune of necessity; overcoming
limitations.**

NAUTHIZ

Need is the oppression of the heart;
yet often it is made by men's sons to help
and heal, however, if they heed it in time.

OERP

ᚾ (Nauthiz): Rune of Restrictions and Resources.

Sound Value: n. (pronounced "Nowth-eez")

Rune order sequence: No. 10.

Literal meaning: Need.

Esoteric meaning: Necessary stress as a goad to self deliverance from distress.

Magickal meaning: "Acknowledging and Removing Limitations".

Divinatory Meaning: Constraints and Suffering; the Wyrd.

Keywords: Necessity; Self-reliance.

Colour: Purple.   **Tree:** Beech/Rowan.

Herb: Snakeroot.   **Element:** Venom.

Associated Diety: The Great Norns (Warders of Orlog).

These are three Etin-Maids. Etins (or Jotnar) are giant preconscious beings whose function is the dissolution of form in nature which is necessary for new form to arise. Thursar and Risar are other names given to the same race. Their names are Urd (that which is), Verdhandi (that which is becoming) and Skuld (that which should be - necessity). They dwell at the foot of the World-Tree Yggdrasil (steed of the terrible one - Odhinn) from which springs the Well of Urd. The West Saxons called it Irminsul (primal pillar).

They dip into the Well's waters (what "is") and sprinkle them mixed with the surrounding clay to sustain the World-Tree. They are it's guardians. If the Tree should die then so would all life in all realms of existence. It is here that the gods gather

121

everyday to hold council. It is said that when the Ragnarok (destruction of the powers) approaches, the Tree will tremble and a man named *Lifthràsir* (thriving remnant) and woman named *Lif* (life) will hide in it to survive the ensuing holocaust.

The Norns shape destiny by weaving the fabric of deeds and time from the yarn spun by the seeress goddess Frigga, wife of Odhinn. This weaving is known as Wyd's Web. The Norns also define Wyrd - the life and death of an individual - by the cutting and staining of runes.

Their Hall is the present where what "is" and what "should be", can be seen. Their animal Fetch (familiar) is the Swan.

Dwelling Hall: Urdarbrunn -   "Urd's Well".

Hall Colour: Rainbow.   **Hall Symbol:** The Swan.

Hall Element: Water.   **Dominant Faculty**: Intuition.

Hall Matters: Psychological health, family, finances, possessions, debts, career, habits, personal motivations, goals, employment, employers.

Need: Analysis.

Attribute: Patient.   **Weakness:** Critical.

Rune Rede for Nauthiz:

Shining Stave - Upright or Unobstructed:

It's time to deal with your wyrd. You find yourself in circumstances that need to be overcome. Your resistance to the situation at hand is generating original thinking, inventiveness and the strength of self-reliance. You realise that only you can break the patterns and restrictions that are fettering your freedom. Your powers of endurance have increased because of your trials. You now see clearly how your present situation came to be, and are now able to use your tenacity to cast off the limitations that once seemed insurmountable. Unused resources offer a means of escape. There is reason to hope.

Shadow Stave - Reversed/Inverted or Obstructed:

Your situation is the wyrd you have made for yourself. Do not continue to make the same mistakes by following the path of least resistance as that would result in further loss of freedom. If your life or present situation is one of drudgery, heavy burdens or severe constraint, look to see how you have imprisoned yourself. Is it by fear, anxiety, guilt, low self-esteem or just lack of effort? Do not be possessive or envious of other people nor blame them for your current situation. People can give advice but only you have the power to initiate action. Generate the internal fires of resistance to your own darkness. Being "fed-up" is the start to finding a solution. Take control of your own life, now, before it is too late!

Nauthiz Key Words:

Shining Stave: Will directed action, resistance against hardship, strength through ordeal, tenacity, original thinking, inventiveness, self-reliance, recognition of the laws of cause and effect, overcoming constraints or limitations, growth through endurance, friction, trouble, bureaucracy.

Shadow Stave: Defeatist attitude, severe constraints on freedom, inability to relieve distress, heavy burdens, drudgery, lack of effort, fears, anxiety, guilt.

Rune 11

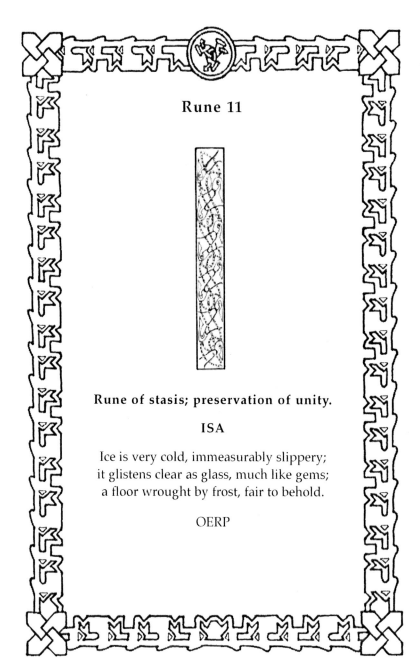

Rune of stasis; preservation of unity.

ISA

Ice is very cold, immeasurably slippery;
it glistens clear as glass, much like gems;
a floor wrought by frost, fair to behold.

OERP

| (Isa): Rune of Reduction and Reinforcement.

Sound Value: i ("ee").   (pronounced "Ees-ar")

Rune order sequence: No. 11.

Literal meaning: Ice.

Esoteric meaning: Unity maintained by concentration of egocentricity.

Magickal meaning: "Isolating the Self to Preserve Integrity".

Divinatory Meaning: Blockages; Grievances; the Skuld.

Keywords: Coagulation; Contraction; Stillness.

Colour: Black.   **Tree:** Alder.

Herb: Henbane.   **Element:** Ice.

Associated Diety: The Goddess Skadi - the "Harmful".

Goddess of winter, revenge, hunting, skiing. Patroness of female warriors. Daughter of the mountain giant Thjazi (self-serving?) who was killed by Thorr. Short-time wife of Njord who selected him as her husband in compensation for her father's death. The choice was made on viewing his beautiful feet - she was not allowed to see his whole body. She mistook him for the god Baldur, son of Odhinn and Frigga. They spent nine nights in each others realms - hers the cold and windy mountains and his the calm and sheltered sea shore. They then separated to their respective realms.

She is one of the Etin (giant) race and aids the Æsir in their revenge on Loki (trickster-god) by placing a serpent above him that drips venom on his face while he lays bound until Ragnarok (destruction of the powers). Loki's wife Sigyn

125

(victory friend) holds out a bowl to catch the venom. His bonds are the entrails of his own son Narvi (narrow?), who was slain by his brother Vali (foreign?) after Thorr and other gods changed him into a wolf.

Her Hall is home for the development of skills for dominant survival. Her animal Fetch (familiar) is the Reindeer.

Dwelling Hall: Thrymheim - "Home of Noise".

Hall Colour: White.   **Hall Symbol:** The Reindeer.

Hall Element: Earth.   **Dominant Faculty:** Feeling.

Hall Matters: Idividuality, psychological privacy, hygiene, enemies, communal service, training, self-employment, employees.

Need: Order.

Attribute: Discriminating.   **Weakness:** Demanding.

Rune Rede for Isa:

Shining Stave - Upright or Unobstructed:

Your ability to withdraw into the self for protection, without losing contact with external events has allowed the formation of a strong personality. This is seen by others as self-control and by yourself as self-worth. This enables you to maintain a unity of purpose in your undertakings, and the ability to control or influence others by your strong will power. Your intuitive sense allows you to jettison attachments to people, places or objects if they are holding you back in your quest for self-determination. Metaphysically, you can enter into deep meditative states where concentration allows transcendental experience without loss of consciousness. Periods of transition in your life may appear to be slow but they will be smooth and the journey only as difficult as you imagine it to be.

Shadow Stave - Reversed/Inverted or Obstructed:

Its time to centre your energies by self-evaluation. This is not the same as self-absorption which can leave you blind to external events. Don't be seduced by the "Status Quo", as this is a defence of ego-centric delusions which are part of the 'herd' mentality and can only lead to loss of true freedom. Suspension of effort leads to loss of will-power and perception of danger. It can result in alienation, not only in society but within your own psyche. Hoarding of skills, emotions or material things can result in entropy, ennui and loneliness leaving you open to manipulation by others. It may be time to let go of your attachments to situations or relationships that give 'illusionary' security. They are constricting you.

Isa Key Words:

Shining Stave: Formation of personality, ego-awareness, unity of purpose, self-control, concentrated will, withdrawal into self for protection without losing contact with external events, ability to influence others, realisation of self-worth, control of others by willpower.

Shadow Stave: Total self-absorption, blindness to external events, lack of inner reserves, loss of will power, suspension of effort, dissipation of power of perception, danger, selfishness, hoarding, alientation, loneliness.

Rune 12

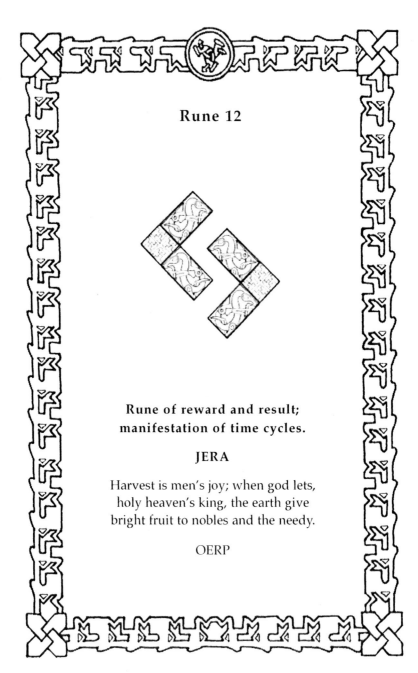

**Rune of reward and result;
manifestation of time cycles.**

JERA

Harvest is men's joy; when god lets,
holy heaven's king, the earth give
bright fruit to nobles and the needy.

OERP

⧊ (Jera): Rune of Profit and Provision.

Sound Value: J [vocalised as "y"]   (pronounced "Yair-ar")

Rune order sequence: No. 12.

Literal meaning: Year (Harvest); Plenty.

Esoteric meaning: Completion of a cycle; Returning to the source; Results of previous actions.

Magickal meaning: "Timing as a Framework for Manifestation".

Divinatory Meaning: Expectations of Success.

Keywords: Turning Point, Reward.

Colour: Green.   **Tree:** Oak/Rowan.

Herb: Rosemary.   **Element:** Earth.

Associated Deity: The Goddess Sif - "Relation".

Mother of the winter archer-god Ullur and wife of the god Thorr. She is a fertility goddess and best known for her long rippling golden hair which was likened to ripe grain swaying in the breeze. The trickster-god Loki, who was envious of her beauty and later boasted of sleeping with her to all the god/esses, cut off her hair which was then likened to the stubble in the field. Thorr threatened to destroy Loki unless he replaced her tresses. Loki approached the Dwarf smiths known as the sons of Ivaldi who fashioned a wig of gold (which adhered to her head and became living hair) to escape Thorr's wrath for his jealous deed.

Ivaldi's sons also magically wrought, at the same time, a ship named Skidbladnir (wooden bladed) for Freyr which was large enough to carry all the gods into battle at Ragnarok (destruction of the powers) but could be folded up like a cloth

129

and carried in a purse; and a spear for Odhinn named Gungnir (swaying one) which was described as strong and slender and always found its mark when cast. These three magical items are symbolic of the intertwining of the life and death mystery.

Her Hall is the dwelling place of the deities of nature. Her animal Fetch (familiar) is a field rodent called the Vole.

Dwelling Hall: Vanaheim -   "Home of Hope".

Hall Colour: Gold.   **Hall Symbol:** The Vole.

Hall Element: Earth.   **Dominant Faculty:** Sensation.

Hall Matters: Long term projects and influences, security, time and nature, evolution, agriculture, endings and beginnings.

Need: Routine.

Attribute: Consideration.   **Weakness:** Vanity.

Rune Rede for Jera:

Shining Stave - Upright or Unobstructed:

Through rational planning and hard work, you have been decisive and your timing has been right. Now you are about to reap the harvest. Abundance in the field of endeavour is the reward for sustained effort. This may not be only material/financial. Harmony with life and pleasure in all activities is a precious state that many work towards. Contentment for those who work with and/or study Flora and Fauna. Delight for lovers and those who nurture children. Flowering and decline are an intrinsic part of natural cycles. You are presently at the pinnacle of this rhythm. Happiness only has value because it is as transient as all states. While you are at peace with the wheel of time, use the positive energy to prepare and sustain you through the inevitable movement into other states and conditions.

For those about to begin long-term projects, begin now. You will have success which will improve your quality of life.

Shadow Stave - Reversed/Inverted or Obstructed:

Your ignorance of natural cycles within your self and nature has lead to a repetition of effort and/or misdirected action. Modern society encourages the over-riding of Bio-rhythms because of the false premise that pausing/rest/contemplation is a waste of "economic time-units". This inevitably leads to fatigue and depletion of energy because without a time of "fallowing", resources do not have time to be renewed. Personally it can result in inadequate planning, wrong timing and lack of results. Internal/external conflict ensues. Learn to pace yourself and work "smart" not "hard" if you wish to see positive results for your efforts. Do not waste your time on relationships, activities or forms of livelihood that are inappropriate to your nature. If you desire economic success but can't achieve it, you are probably and chronically looking for the "fast Buck". If you are self-indulgent or frivolous, you only reap what you sow.

Jera Key Words:

Shining Stave: Rewards for right effort, cyclical development, fruition, eternal renewal, turning point, good timing, abundance, prosperity, harmony, financial affairs, farming activities, seasonal and biological rhythms.

Shadow Stave: Repetition, lessons not learnt, misdirected effort, bad timing, inability to "tune in", poverty, internal and external conflict, ignorance of nature.

Rune 13

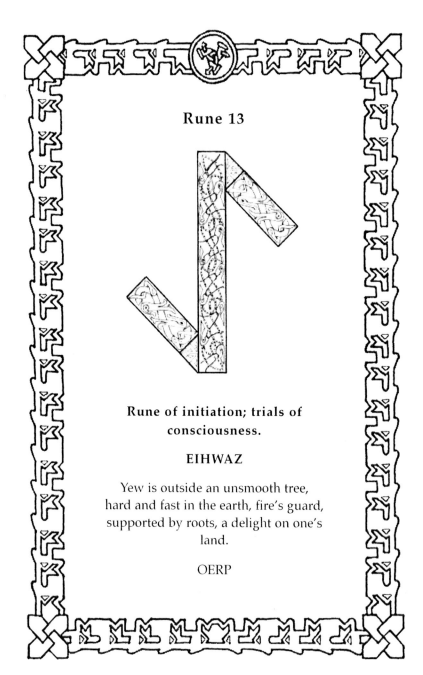

Rune of initiation; trials of consciousness.

EIHWAZ

Yew is outside an unsmooth tree, hard and fast in the earth, fire's guard, supported by roots, a delight on one's land.

OERP

∫ (Eihwaz): Rune of Endurance and Exploration.

Sound Value: ei. [vocalised as in German "ein"] (pronounced "eye-varz" or "ay-varz")

Rune order sequence: No. 13.

Literal meaning: Yew Tree.

Esoteric meaning: The human spine as the internal cognate to the World Tree called 'Yggdrasil' - containing access to the spiritual worlds through the psycho-somatic centers called Hvels (wheels, ie. chakra).

Magickal meaning: "Initiating a free flow of consciousness within the Psyche".

Divinatory Meaning: Motivation to Excel.

Keywords: Hardiness; Flexibility.

Colour: Red.　　　**Tree:** Yew/Ash.

Herb: Bryony.　　　**Element:** Fire.

Associated Diety: The God Ullur - the "Brilliant One" or "Glorious".

The Archer god. God of winter, patron of hunters and single combatants, skiers and skaters. Son of the star-being Orvandil (high apart?) and Sif, Thorr's wife, stepson to Thorr. Also nephew to Idunna (goddess of spring) and Baldur's wife Nanna (mamma?) He is called upon to witness oaths. He may have been at one time even more prominent than Odhinn as one tradition recalls that Odhinn offered Ullur's favours to any one who would help him. He is one of the Vaniric gods. His hall is home of the Yew tree whose wood makes the best bows.

133

The yew, an evergreen, is also associated with endurance/ survival of the body through winter hardship and especially of the soul after death. It was only used for winter fires in the severest conditions owing to its slow burning qualities and intense heat radiation. The Vitkis (sorcerer/shamans) would meditate under its canopy in summer to breathe the trees' resinating fumes which are toxic enough to induce visionary states and out-of-body experiences. The Yew tree was planted in burial grounds in heathen times. This tradition was carried through into the christian period.

His Hall is the place where the boundary of experience is pushed to its furthermost frontier. His Fetch animal (familiar) is the Bear.

Dwelling Hall: Ydalir - "Yew Dale".

Hall Colour: Gold.   **Hall Symbol:** The Bear.

Hall Element: Water.   **Dominant Faculty:** Intuition.

Hall Matters: Philosophy, idealism, psychic experiences. Foreign places. Science, technology, inventions.

Need: Freedom.

Attribute: Optimistic.   **Weakness:** Callousness.

Rune Rede for Eihwaz:

Shining Stave - Upright or Unobstructed:

Your desire for self-understanding (and your place in the cosmic scheme) has overcome the fear of the "unknown" and you now delve freely into the realms of the unconscious/superconscious. By perception of the linkage of the Self to the pulses of the Multiversal realms, you are awakening to your conscious purpose in this life. This generates motivation and strengthens the will. It is self initiation into the mysteries of consciousness, where you perceive the ebb and flow of psychic energy through your self and the external universe. It is your protection from chaotic forces. This understanding allows flexibility in dealing with the vicissitudes of life. Discipline is needed to maintain the stamina to not only pass through these experiences, but to grasp the complexity of the human and non-human realms, without being overwhelmed. In everyday life, your perception of other peoples drives/motivations allows you deal with them openly and not become over-stressed by any situation.

Shadow Stave - Reversed/Inverted or Obstructed:

You are being held back by self defeating thoughts or habits of which you may not be conscious. Know that the Universe, through the laws of manifestation responds to all thoughts and actions within the Web of Wyrd. You create your own reality. Rigidity to the fluctuations of consciousness can cause confusion, weakness and a retreat from trials. This can, in turn, generate fear which attracts negative and/or chaotic experiences which may lead to psychic gullibility and misdirected goals. Do not attempt to delve into the occult, ie. hidden realms, unless you are prepared to nurture and direct the energy of consciousness that will be unleashed. Unused, it can cause profound personality disturbance. Uncontrolled, it can lead to a "breakdown" and psychosis. If you are dealing with others who are disturbed, avoid becoming embroiled in their chaos. Leave them to be helped by those who have been prepared through training or experience .

Eihwaz Key Words:

Shining Stave: Unconscious drive, conscious purpose, motivation, numinous awakening, endurance, strengthened will, awareness of other realities, psychic and spiritual expansion through occult practice, revelation and vision, protection from chaotic forces, magick, flexibility, mysticism.

Shadow Stave: Retreat from trials, confusion, weakness, fear of death, dissatisfaction, being held back by self defeating thoughts or habits, neurosis, loss of flexibility, misdirected goals, psychic gullibility.

Rune 14

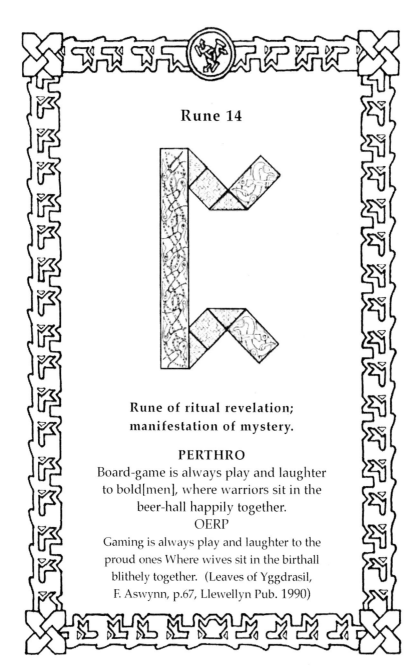

**Rune of ritual revelation;
manifestation of mystery.**

PERTHRO

Board-game is always play and laughter
to bold[men], where warriors sit in the
beer-hall happily together.

OERP

Gaming is always play and laughter to the
proud ones Where wives sit in the birthall
blithely together. (Leaves of Yggdrasil,
F. Aswynn, p.67, Llewellyn Pub. 1990)

꘡ (Perthro): Rune of Ritual and Release.

Sound Value: p.   (pronounced "Purth-roh")

Rune order sequence: No. 14.

Literal meaning: Music and Dance, Gaming.

Esoteric meaning: Ritual practices. Divination to indicate Orlog; the Well of Wyrd.

Magickal meaning: "Accessing Hamingja - the hidden store of power and luck".

Divinatory Meaning: Release of Tension through Fortuitous Events.

Keywords: Revelation, Luck, Opportunity .

Colour: Orange-Red.   **Tree:** Beech.

Herb: Aconite.   **Element:** Yeast.

Associated Diety: The Goddess Frigga - " Lady" - 'the All-Mother'.

Her name is not directly related to the English slang word, though the two derive from the same original root (love, pleasure). Known as the "Silent Seeress" and Hlin (protectress), she is the Great Mother. She has a handmaiden called Fulla (abundance) and a messenger named Gna (plenty?). As wife of Odhinn she shares his High Seat over-looking the Nine Worlds. She is patron goddess of the home and married women's mysteries including traditional crafts (spinning, weaving, cooking, sewing) and associated magick. She is called on for protection of women in childbirth and to protect children, especially sons going to war. Frigga is the mother of Baldur (bold), who was slain by his blind brother

Hodur (warrior) through the treachery of the Loki, and is often thought of as still mourning for him.

Her especial function is to keep social order even to the point of resisting the will of Odhinn. She has direct knowledge of the wyrd (destiny) of the universe through her connection to the Norns (goddesses of cosmic law) for whom she spins the yarn of Orlog (primal layers of thought and deed). She is also a shape-shifter taking the form of a Falcon. While her name has the same meaning as the goddess Freyja, she should not be mistaken for her as they have polar though complimentary functions as deities. She is the mother/wife while Freyja is the warrior/lover.

Her Hall is the place of collective ancestral values. Her animal Fetch (familiar) is the Falcon.

Dwelling Hall: Fensalir -   "Marsh Halls".

Hall Colour: Dark Blue.   **Hall Symbol:** The Falcon.

Hall Element: Water.   **Dominant Faculty:** Intuition.

Hall Matters: Ritual feasting, ancestral knowledge, occult secrets, women's mysteries, childbirth, sex magic, speculation, gambling.

Need: Communality.

Attribute: Trusting.   **Weakness:** Vindictive.

Rune Rede for Perthro:

Shining Stave - Upright or Unobstructed:

Past life wisdom, knowledge and hamingja are available to you. With this comes the awareness of your strengths, weaknesses, rewards and debts. Just as important is the certainty of your power to weave the wyrd for your own benefit. Pushing your luck against the odds is more than chance. It is knowing your own potential and feeling out of the probability factors then acting on intuitive pulsations with courage, and a certain sense of detachment - win or lose you are still increasing your power of opportunity. The use of your psychic faculties is increasing - the power of clairvoyance for divination and helping others is strong. You are invited to join the "spiritual warriors" who drink the "Mead of Inspiration". Fellowship, good times, mysterious encounters and serendipity that may change your life for the better are indicated. A release of tension through entertainment, fun and games is in the offering - enjoy! For some women - an unexpected pregnancy. For those already pregnant, a time to explore and enjoy the altered state of your hormonal reality and to bond with your family and support network. If giving birth is imminent then celebrate it as the holy event that it is.

Shadow Stave - Reversed/Inverted or Obstructed:

Your life is full of potential yet you are unaware of it. You are like a woman who is pregnant but is not in tune enough with her own body to recognise the fact. A certain shallowness of character, at the present time, is making you virtually blind to the opportunities that are presenting to you. You take impulsive/uncalculated risks without concern for the possible repercussions. You are in danger of being overwhelmed by events that should be foreseen, but aren't, because of your indulgence/attachment to life's distractive sensual pleasures. You realise that their pursuit does not relieve the bottled-up tension you continually feel. You are stagnating because of a lack of purpose/life direction - you don't as yet know why you are here and therefore are unable to consciously evolve. Time to do some serious "soul-searching". Consult the runes for their rede - and have the courage to act on it. For some divorce/separation or a period of solitude is imminent and necessary. Pregnant women must pay particular attention to their health - seek out your midwife or doctor; and spend more time with other mothers, just for company and

140

relaxation. Learn that the way to fulfilment is by consciously recognising the window of opportunity and acting on it, not just wishful thinking - this is so called "good luck".

Perthro Key Words:

Shining Stave: Rune wisdom, recovery of hidden knowledge, hidden talents, that which is about to manifest, evolutionary change, knowledge of cause and effect, occult abilities, the feminine mysteries, fellowship and good times, good omen, happiness, luck, entertainment, release of tension.

Shadow Stave: Lack of foresight, over-indulgence in life's pleasures, addiction, wasting of vital force, dissipation, being overwhelmed by your Wyrd, uneasiness, tension, stagnation, unhappiness, solitude, divorce.

Rune 15

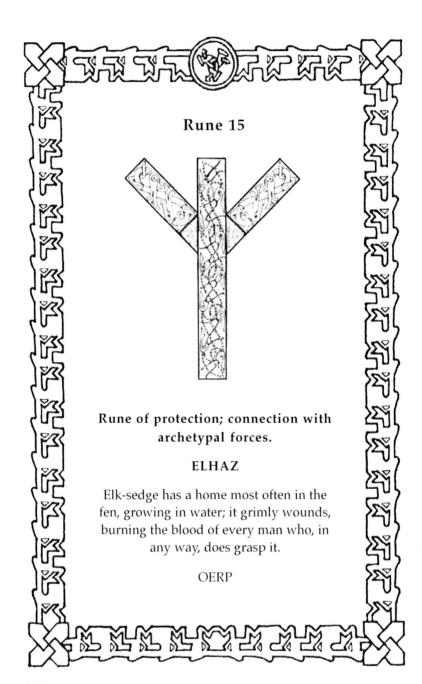

Rune of protection; connection with archetypal forces.

ELHAZ

Elk-sedge has a home most often in the
fen, growing in water; it grimly wounds,
burning the blood of every man who, in
any way, does grasp it.

OERP

ᛦ (Elhaz): Rune of Defence and Assistance.

Sound Value: z. (pronounced "Airlh-arz")

Rune order sequence: No. 15.

Literal meaning: Elk, Temple as Sanctuary.

Esoteric meaning: Warding and Connecting force.

Magickal meaning: "Appropriate Action through Evolutionary Impetus".

Divinatory Meaning: Maintenance of Position.

Keywords: Support; Earned Safety .

Colour: Silver.   **Tree:** Yew/Service.

Herb: Sedge.   **Element:** Water.

Associated Deity: The God Heimdall - The "Home Brightener ".

He is known as Vindlher (watchman), guardian of the three stranded (air, fire and water) Rainbow bridge between Midgard (Earth) and Asgard (Heaven) called Bifrost (shimmering path). The protector of those seeking higher consciousness.

In the form of Rig (king), Heimdall was the progenitor and instructor of the three classes of people in society - servants, freeman and rulers. He is the spiritual mediator between the two realms and the god of intellect, learning, teaching. He taught Odhinn's Runes to mankind.

At the time of Ragnarok (the final conflict between the forces of Order and Chaos) he will blow the Gjollarhorn (resounding horn) to warn the gods of the approaching danger and call

143

them to battle. This horn is a Ram's and is said that it is kept in Mimir's (mindfulness) well. Heimdall is also known as Hallingskidi (asymetrically horned), another association with the Ram. The horn's name also means 'horn of the river Gjoll'. This river of blood is one that flows from the underworld, whence much wisdom is said to derive.

His Hall is the storehouse of spiritual knowledge upon which civilisation is formed. His animal Fetch (familiar) is the Ram.

Hall Dwelling: Himminbjorg -   "Heaven Mountain".

Hall Colour: Silver.   **Hall Symbol:** The Ram.

Hall Element: Air.   **Dominant Faculty:** Thought.

Hall Matters: Safety, shelter, sanctuaries, security, station in society, religion, occult, psychological states.

Need: Guidance.

Attribute: Idiosyncratic.   **Weakness:** Superficiality.

Rune Rede for Elhaz:

Shining Stave - Upright or Unobstructed:

You are awakening to your supra-mundane identity. With this comes the ability to contact the realms where your more subtle bodies, or levels of mind, function without reference to sensual stimulation. These planes or dimensions are dwelling places of spiritual entities some discarnate, others personifications of natural forces - the highest being the god/esses who are both internal (archetypes) and external beings (ie. they have self awareness). Through this contact, whether through dreams, visions, portents or meditation, you have guidance, protection and psychological comfort while seeking the sources of your own magickal power. A philosopical understanding of sociological structuring enables you to connect with those who will reinforce your present security. You know your position and can now gain support from benefactors; if you acknowledge your responsibilities and trust in their guidance and goodwill while working towards your personal goals. Listen to your peers in regards to these matters.

Shadow Stave - Reversed/Inverted or Obstructed:

There is hidden danger in your approach to reality. You may be feeling a loss of spiritual connection and psychic disturbance. Psychically, this rune position is a warning not to explore supernatural experiences in a flippant way, such as through drugs. You may be unprepared or even unwilling to accept the existence of realities beyond the input from your physical senses. You may also refuse to believe that there is more to yourself than just the personality/ego. This can be reflected in the non-acknowledgment of other peoples complexities, even their right to hold views/philosophies or beliefs different from your own. This attitude can lead to a loss of support from those who have previously guided you either from the subtle realms or in everyday life. Beware of betrayal from authorities and "friends". Maybe you are mixing with the wrong crowd - those who do not understand you and thus feel threatened by your different values and sociological comphrehension. Be prepared and very wary in dealing with unfamiliar people or situations - their actions could result in long lasting (and sometimes permanent) trauma. Grabbing after any form of power through greed can result in severe loss.

Elhaz Key Words:

Shining Stave: Expansion, spiritual guidance, awakening, protective force and/or enclosure, religious comfort, willed communication with non-human beings, knowledge of "right" spiritual practices, higher life, increase of magickal power. Support from benefactors.

Shadow Stave: Loss of divine support/link, hidden danger from chaotic forces, both external and internal, fall from "grace", consumption by archetypal psychic forces, loss of spiritual integration due to lack of preparation, betrayal by supporters, endings.

Rune 16

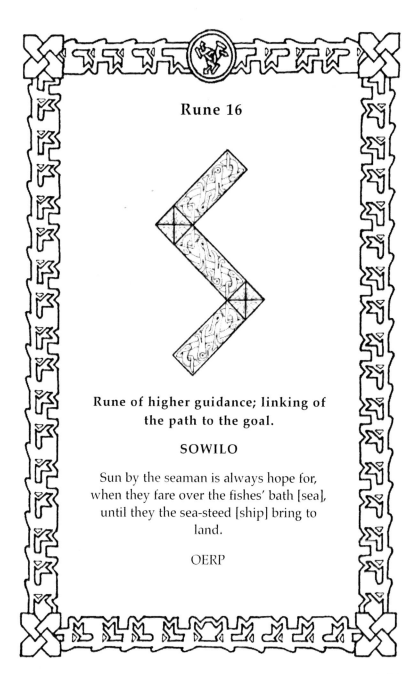

Rune of higher guidance; linking of the path to the goal.

SOWILO

Sun by the seaman is always hope for, when they fare over the fishes' bath [sea], until they the sea-steed [ship] bring to land.

OERP

ৢ (Sowilo): Rune of Discrimination and Determination.

Sound Value: s.   (pronounced "So-will-oh")

Rune order sequence: No. 16.

Literal meaning: The Sun (the Solar Wheel).

Esoteric meaning: Guidance and protection during the souls' evolution; dissipation of ignorance.

Magickal meaning: "Removing Illusions and Obstructions to Advancement".

Divinatory Meaning: Accelerated Development and Independence.

Keywords: Intent; Optimism, Breakthrough.

Colour: White.   **Tree:** Juniper / Bay.

Herb: Sage / Aconite.   **Element:** Salt

Associated Diety: The Goddess Sunna.

Also known as Sol by the Vikings. The personification of the Sun which is feminine in Germanic lore. She is the daughter of Mundilfari (turner?) and the brother of Mani (the Moon). Sunna is said to be the manifested (material) eye of Odhinn, just as her brother Mani represents Odhinn's other (spiritual) eye which he sacrified into Mimir's (mindfulness) Well for the gaining of wisdom. Sunna drives a fiery chariot across the sky drawn by a horse named Skinfaxi (shining mane) and is pursued by a wolf-shaped troll (magical being) named Skoll (treachery) from the place called Iron Wood in the land of the giants (Jotunheim). Skoll will devour her at Ragnarok (destruction of the powers) which is the final battle between the forces of order and chaos.

148

Another name given to Sunna is Alfrodul (elf-beam) and alludes to her connection with the realm of the Light-Elves, magical beings (and sometimes ancestors) that live in the higher mental dimensions and give guidance/inspiration to those in Midgard (the Earth-Realm). They are also said to be the shapers of the sun's power that preserves all life on earth and ride sunbeams down to the earth.

Her Hall is the source of the collective folk-soul's driving force of evolution. Her animal Fetch (familiar) is the Eagle.

Dwelling Hall: Vindvefja -   "Wind Weaver".

Hall Colour: Light Blue.   **Hall Symbol:** The Eagle.

Hall Element: Fire.   **Dominant Faculty:** Feeling.

Hall Matters: Self-worth, spiritual evolution, guidance, leadership, education, philanthropy, consumption.

Need: Committment.

Attribute: Sincerity.   **Weakness:** Argumentative.

Rune Rede for Sowilo:

Shining Stave - Upright or Unobstructed:

Whether your question involves your life journey or a particular goal, know that your will and charisma can break inertia and remove all obstacles. This rune's energy dissolves illusion and offers protection to yourself and those in your care. Stick to your goal until you have won through. Fixed concentration on the task will attract guidance through good advice and assistance. Success for those involved with education/study of any subject, whether student or tutor. Quick learning and honour in all undertakings. Accelerated healing ability through access to right counsel and methods of treatment. Metaphysically, you have activated your psychic energy centres (Wheels, Chakram) thus accelerating your spiritual recognition and access to the subtle realms of existence. Magickal evolution is the result.

Shadow Stave - Reversed/Inverted or Obstructed:

Your loss of purpose and/or lack of direction has left you gullible to bad or wrong advice. If you are weak willed or immature, you can be easily mislead in pursuit of wrong goals or those set by others for their benefit, not yours. You have the tendency to do the same to others, so sometimes it is the case of the "conman" getting "conned". Your present situation and/or state of mind may seduce you into taking dishonourable short cuts which will take you even further from your path - both in the world or in spirit. Grand goals are worthy to work towards but you must take responsibility to take one step at a time otherwise you will lose interest. Do thorough research on your choices. Seek advice from proven, reliable authorities and follow it.

Sowilo Key Words:

Shining Stave: Revealed direction, spiritual force, journey, the right path, the right goal, dynamic evolution, magickal evolution, fixed concentration, success and honour in all undertakings, dissipation of all obstacles, breaking of inertia, quick learning, luck, healing, achievement, victory through will, strengthening of psychic centres (wheels, chakras) in body, education, tutors, hope, protection.

Shadow Stave: Weak-willed, easily led, bad advice being taken, pursuit of wrong goals or those set by others, gullibility, lack of direction, loss of purpose, achievements gained through dishonourable means.

Chapter Nine
Tyr's Aett

Learn victory runes   If thou victory wantest,
and have them on they sword's hilt -
on thy sword's hilt some,   on thy sword's guard some
and call twice upon Tyr.

(The Lay of Sigdrifa - Poetic Edda)

Rune 17

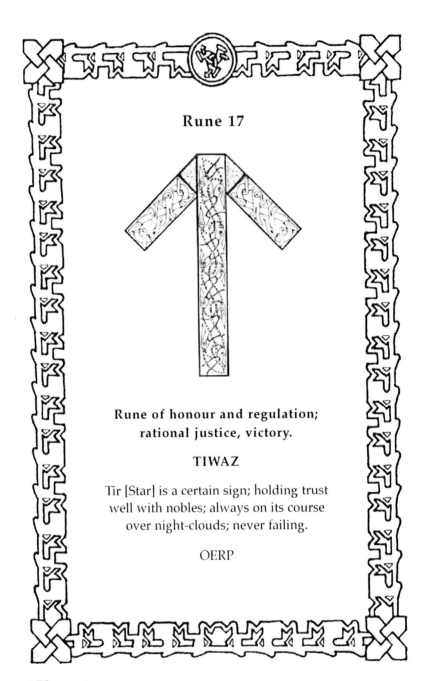

**Rune of honour and regulation;
rational justice, victory.**

TIWAZ

Tir [Star] is a certain sign; holding trust
well with nobles; always on its course
over night-clouds; never failing.

OERP

↑ (Tiwaz): Rune of Law and Order.

Sound Value: t. (pronounced "Tee-varz")

Rune order sequence: No. 17.

Literal meaning: The god Tyr.

Esoteric meaning: The functioning of Natural Law in the individual and society.

Magickal meaning: "Asserting Authority to Gain and Maintain Control".

Divinatory Meaning: Honourable Conduct.

Keywords: Justice, Victory, Sacrifice.

Colour: Indigo.   **Tree:** Oak/Ash.

Herb: Mistletoe.   **Element:** Iron.

Associated Diety: Tyr -"heavenly", "god".

He may have been the Germanic equivalent of the Indo-European "Sky-Father". He is known to have had a feminine twin called Cisa or Zisa (goddess; earth-mother?). He is the warrior God of Justice and is associated with the "Thing" (law council) where the battle of individuals or factions is sublimated into a form where the process solves the problem in a way which helps the whole community rather than harms it. If necessary, force of arms will be used to establish order. He is known as "One-handed" because he sacrificed his hand in the mouth of the Fenris Wolf to aid in Fenrir's (marsh dweller) binding by the Æsir gods.

Loki spawned this wolf - who will devour Odhinn at Ragnarok (destruction of the powers) - and left him in the care of the Æsir. As he grew larger and more ferocious, none of the gods would feed and tend him except for Tyr. The gods became afraid of Fenrir and tried to bind him with chains which he broke on all occassions. Finally the gods had a magickal fetter name Gleipnir (open one) made by the dwarfs. Tyr placed the fetter on Fenrir on behalf of the gods. He tricked the wolf into believing it a test of strength. Fenrir accepted the dare on the condition that Tyr place his hand in Fenrir's mouth as a surety of good faith. On realising he was unable to get free, the wolf snapped off Tyr's hand. Tyr will fight the guardian-hound of Hel, Garm (rag), at Ragnarok.

His Hall is the place of balance between the ego and the collective conscious. His animal Fetch (familiar) is the Wolf.

Dwelling Hall: Asgardr -   "Enclosure of the Æsir".

Hall Colour: Dark Blue.   **Hall Symbol:** The Wolf.

Hall Element: Air.   **Dominant Faculty**: Thought.

Hall Matters: Ambition, authority, responsibilities, legal affairs, disputes, war.

Need: Understanding.

Attribute: Courage.   **Weakness:** Fickleness.

Rune Rede for Tiwaz:

Shining Stave - Upright or Unobstructed:

Victory is yours by keeping disciplined through the hard times. Be rational in your approach to important matters. Analysis of situations may call for the sacrifice of some of your, or the group's, desires in order to achieve an honourable solution. Being methodical is the key to success. Your initiative makes you a leader whom others look up to when difficult decisions must be made, knowing that you always weigh the consequences before committing yourself and others. You can also be the champion of the "underdog" if you give and keep loyalty. Your religious instinct and sense of justice can act as a

154

unifying principle among all classes of people. Success in martial and legal matters and social reform. Don't be afraid to fight for your rights and the rights of others.

Shadow Stave - Reversed/Inverted or Obstructed:

You may be suffering from loss of authority. Injustice and disorder may surround you, from personal harassment to persecution from the Law system or other powerful institutions. You have lost your perspective on the situations that are troubling you. It may be that you are being short-sighted and irrational in your planning or expectations. Learn to compromise while holding true to your ideals. Nothing can be gained from over-sacrifice unless you are seeking pity and desire to be known as a "martyr" . The worst possible reaction would be for you to act like a cornered beast and lash out at friend and foe alike because of frustration. Be careful of loss through "burn-out". If you can't win, retreat and live to fight another day!

Tiwaz Key Words:

Shining Stave: Faith, loyalty, religious instinct, social regulation, spiritual discipline, divine law and order, initiative, leadership, hero, champion, martial strength, victory through "right" action, protection through law, honourable action, rational order, intellectual analysis, exactitude, precision, methodicity, building of will, legal matters, unifying principle, scientific analysis.

Shadow Stave: Injustice, short-sightedness, imbalance, over-analysis, irrationality, loss of authority, disorder and strife, confusion, "burn out" through over-sacrifice, mental limitation, fettered action, defeat.

Rune 18

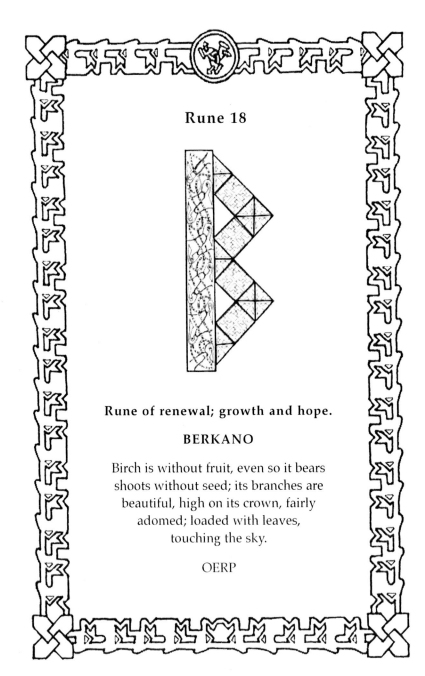

Rune of renewal; growth and hope.

BERKANO

Birch is without fruit, even so it bears
shoots without seed; its branches are
beautiful, high on its crown, fairly
adorned; loaded with leaves,
touching the sky.

OERP

ᛒ (Berkano): Rune of Conservation and Continuity.

Sound Value: b.   (pronounced "Burk-arn-oh")

Rune order sequence: No. 18.

Literal meaning: Birch; Berchta/Pertcha - The Goddess of Spring.

Esoteric meaning: The birth/death/rebirth cycle; The present moment.

Magickal meaning: "Containing and Utilising the Collective Integrity ".

Divinatory Meaning: Renewal of an Enterprise.

Keywords: Containment; Conservation; Continuity; Renewal .

Colour: Green.   **Tree:** Birch/Poplar.

Herb: Lady's Mantle.   **Element:** Earth.

Associated Diety: The Goddess Idunna - the "Rejuvenator".

The Goddess of Spring. She is of a race of gods even older than the Vanir (fertility gods) and personifies the essence of the female principle, just as the god Ing-Freyr personifies the male principle. In this she has close associations with the goddess Freyja. Idunna is known to be care free and untroubled by the passing of time. She is daughter of Ivalde (a star being), the sister of Nanna (mamma), Baldur's wife, and Orvandil (high apart?) and the wife of Bragi (Poetry). Idunna is the custodian of the golden apples that the Æsir gods consume to maintain their eternal youth. Apples are one of the holiest symbols of life and rebirth among the Germanic folk, often appearing as graves gifts since the early Bronze Age.

Idun, along with her precious apples, was tricked by the god Loki into the hands of the giant Thjazi (self-serving?), the father of the goddess Skadi (harm) who, disguised as an eagle, kidnapped her. As the gods began to age and wither, Loki was forced on pain of mutilation to rescue and return her. He borrowed Freyja's (Frigga's?) falcon skin and flew to Thrymheim (place of din). There he changed Idunna into the form of a nut and carried her and her apples back home. The nut is another symbol of rejuvenation and rebirth. Thjazi chased them in his eagle form but was incinerated as he reached the walls of Asgard. The god/esses quickly ate the golden apples and were restored to their former beauty and power. At Ragnarok (destruction of the powers) Idunna will sink below the roots of the World Tree (Yggdrasil) to re-emerge in the new world.

Her Hall is the place of maternal nurturing and growth. Her animal Fetch (familiar) is the Beaver.

Dwelling Hall: Idavoll - "Place of Splendour".

Hall Colour: Gold.   **Hall Symbol:** The Beaver.

Hall Element: Earth.   **Dominant Faculty**: Sensation.

Hall Matters: Feminine influence and projection, pregnancy, motherhood, family health, children, the aged.

Need: Introspection.

Attribute: Dutiful.   **Weakness:** Inhibited.

Rune Rede for Berkano:

Shining Stave - Upright or Unobstructed:

After a quiet or seemingly static time, things are once again on the move. Changes will be gradual but ultimately rewarding. Old loves and ties are strengthened and family life is pleasant. For some, there is or has been a period of self-containment/

withdrawal where transformation, eg. recovery from illness or creative unfoldment, such as craft skills, occurred in secret. Periods of service to the community/clan have taught you the importance of patience as a tool of learning. For others, pregnancy, births and/or the dedication to nurturing children or elderly folk has been a quiet focus for some time. All these experiences have been integrated and now you are ready to blossom in your own right. This is a time to realise that all reality resides in the present moment. Those of a contemplative nature have realised that the unbroken line of ancestral wisdom concerning the cycles of nature - birth/death/rebirth - provides a foundation for renewed growth.

Shadow Stave - Reversed/Inverted or Obstructed:

Loss of conscious clarity is causing you to retreat from life's challenges. You are in a period of hibernation. If there are feelings of sterility, then you are not using your time of withdrawal to the best advantage. If you suffer from a withering of hope, then you are cut off from your spiritual roots. Loss of family support, emotional estrangement, domestic friction and even death may be a part of your present experience. Grief over loss is natural but be wary of wallowing in self pity. Observe nature and see that nothing remains permanently in any state. Only humans who mistakenly see themselves outside natural cycles try to fix things in a static condition. You must accept what you cannot control. Grasp the present moment; it is all you have! Spring always follows winter - nurture yourself for renewal.

Berkano Key Words:

Shining Stave: Collection, Self-containment,   secrecy, womb, shelter, women's mysteries, maternity, fertility, sexuality, new beginnings based on tradition, becoming, birth/ death/rebirth cycle, awakening, awareness of the moment, beauty, domestic tranquility, fruition, creative unfoldment, concealment, hidden transformation, growth, protection, collection and conservation.

Shadow Stave: Scattering, loss of conscious clarity, retreat, sterility, withering of growth, stagnation, cut off from "roots", loss of family support, estrangement, domestic friction, death.

Rune 19

**Rune of harmony and trust;
self-discilpine.**

EHWAZ

War-horse is, before earls, the joy of
nobles, a horse proud of hooves, when
the warriors around, wealthy in steeds,
exchange speech; and is, to the restless,
ever a comfort.

OERP

ᛗ (Ehwaz): Rune of Instinct and Adjustment.

Sound Value: e. (vocalised as in "end")

(pronounced "Air-varz")

Rune order sequence: No. 19.

Literal meaning: Horse.

Esoteric meaning: Yoking within of masculine/feminine principles for spiritual growth; Control of the body through discipline.

Magickal meaning: "Maintaining Co-ordination during Psychological Transistions".

Divinatory Meaning: Messages and Messengers.

Keywords: Co-ordination, Union, Harmony.

Colour: Orange-Gold.   **Tree:** Ash/Elm.

Herb: Ragwort.   **Element:** Yeast.

Associated Diety: The Valkyries - "Choosers of the Slain".

These are feminine spirits that acts as both psychopomps (guides of the dead) and guardians of the living. They ride above the battlefield to choose the warriors who are to fall and protect those to whom they are going to give victory. They are closely associated with Odhinn but are led by Freyja who has first choice of the slain who go to her hall, Folkvang (field of the warrior folk). The remainder are taken to Valholl (hall of the slain) in Asgard (enclosure of the æsir) which is under Odhinn's juristiction. Within Valholl, they also act as serving maids at the table to these heroes called Einherjar (lone fighters) whose job is now to prepare for the final battle between order and chaos, Ragnarok (destruction of the powers).

They are closely related to and may be cognate with the Fetches (*Fylgjur*, ON) guardian spirits that attache themselves to individuals, often from birth, and remain with them till death and sometimes beyond. They may also choose to transfer their attention to other family members. They usually only show themselves, with a warning, to the individual or their close associates in time of crisis and can appear either as an animal (familiar) or a woman. This may be either in the waking or dream state. They may also be called *Disir* (ON) - the guardian goddesses of families).

Their Hall is the place where personality and essential spirit are integrated. Their Fetch (familiar) is the Horse.

Dwelling Hall: Valholl -   "Hall of the Slain".

Hall Colour: Red.   **Hall Symbol:** The Horse.

Hall Element: Air.   **Dominant Faculty:** Thought.

Hall Matters: Psychological integrity and adaptability, partnerships, marriage, precognition, astral experiences, vehicles of travel, journeys.

Need: Trust.

Attribute: Loyalty.   **Weakness:** Co-dependent.

Rune Rede for Ehwaz:

Shining Stave - Upright or Unobstructed:

Success is indicated in all partnership arrangements where teamwork and close co-operation are essential. You generate trust and loyalty because of empathic understanding. Rapid progress in achieving goals especially in personal/emotional relationships and business arrangements. Work to acquire a

163

balance between the masculine and feminine perspective in any given situation. This can be expressed as left/right brain equilibrium in thought, ie. rational/intuitional - analytical/instinctual. Nurture the harmony of the above within yourself through fulfilment of emotional/physical needs. Focused exercise and relaxation allow the body to become a powerful vehicle to accomplish your needs. Encourage others to do the same. You have access to the reservoir of past life memories and talents. This is the rune of shamanic journeys, a part of the magickal craft of Seidhr (shamanism). The horse is a symbol of your own ability to travel within the subtle realms in a thought body of your own creation. Internal journeys generate self acceptance, healing and wisdom. External journeys bring satisfaction through co-operative adventure.

Shadow Stave - Reversed/Inverted or Obstructed:

If you sense disharmony or deceit in your relationships either personal or business, the source may be duplication of effort. Let go of a dominating attitude and trust others to be self aware and competent. If you find yourself in competition with others who are close to you, ask them why they think it necessary to "outshine" you. Ask yourself the same question. Our present society holds competitiveness as a supreme virtue as it brings about greater effort but if it masks greed and/or low self-esteem, then we tend to replace trust with paranoia and continually look for signs of betrayal. Are you operating from instinctual drives or from wholistic observation? This can apply to any situation whether within the family, social group or business. On the other side, avoid slipping into co-dependant relationships which can lead to a blurring of self identity. You give away your power and them blame others for your non-fulfilment. This can result in break up of marriages, friendships and business arrangements. Come to terms with your own needs then dealing with others will be less of a problem. Unexpected journeys and/or forced relocation are indicated.

164

Ehwaz Key Words:

Shining Stave: Teamwork, trust, loyalty, complementary forces, telepathic linkage, internal guidance, astral vehicle (vehicle of soul travel), sensuality, fertility, close cooperation, relationships, partnerships, marriage, peace, sympathy, integrated magickal protection, swiftness, journeys, prophecy.

Shadow Stave: Duplication of effort, deceit, betrayal, mistrust, disharmony, divorce, unplanned travel, psychic disturbance.

Rune 20

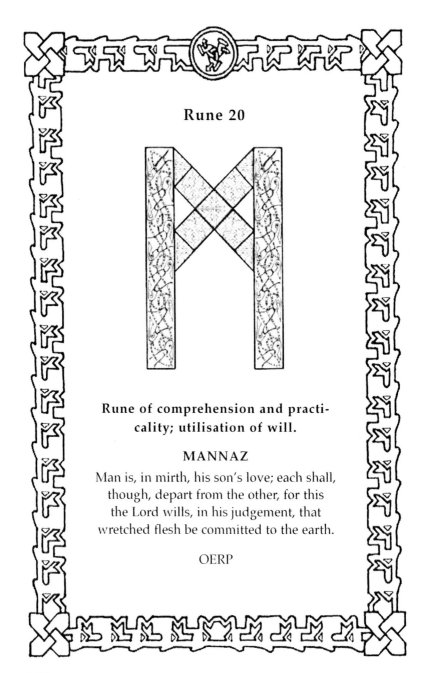

Rune of comprehension and practicality; utilisation of will.

MANNAZ

Man is, in mirth, his son's love; each shall,
though, depart from the other, for this
the Lord wills, in his judgement, that
wretched flesh be committed to the earth.

OERP

ᛗ (Mannaz): Rune of Acceptance and Pragmatism.

Sound Value: m.   (pronounced "Marn-arz")

Rune order sequence: No. 20.

Literal meaning: Man (Mankind - Human Being). Divine Ancestor.

Esoteric meaning: The true nature of humanity - both beast and god.

Magickal meaning: "Superseding the Limitations of Nature".

Divinatory Meaning: Adaption to the Realities of Life .

Keywords: Self-consciousness, Reality, Utilisation.

Colour: Silver.   **Tree:** Holy.

Herb: Madder.   **Element:** Salt.

Associated Diety: The God Mimir - "mindful/memory wise".

A mystic figure of ancestral tribal wisdom. He is of the giant race also known as Etins who sometimes dwelt with the Æsir - the brother of Odhinn's Etin-mother Bestla (bark?). At the end of the primal war between the Æsir (gods of self-consciousness) and the Vanir (gods of natural instinct), he was sent as a peace hostage to the Vanir along with Odhinn's taciturn brother Hoenir. When they discovered that Hoenir (self?) could not act without the advice of Mimir (mindful/memory?), they decapitated Mimir and sent his head back to Odhinn (inspiration). Odhinn preserved the head with herbs and spells and consults the disembodied Mimir for advice. His head rests besides one of the wells under the roots of the World-Tree, also known as Laeràd (counsel yielder) in Jotunheim (home of the giants) called Mimir's Well .

Odin sacrificed an eye in to this well to gain Mimir's vision of past and future. It is said that Odhinn also drinks daily from the well by using Heimdall's, the Watchman god, ram's-horn, the Gjollarhorn (resounding horn) which is left there to be guarded by Mimir until it is needed to summon the gods for Ragnarok (destruction of the powers). Heimdall's horn is a symbol of mankind's origin in the animal world.

Mimir's Hall is the place where mankind knows his collective past, true nature and potential. His Fetch animal (familiar) is the Hawk.

Dwelling Hall: Mimisbrunn -   "Mimir's Well".

Hall Colour: Blue.   **Hall Symbol:** The Hawk.

Hall Element: Air.   **Dominant Faculty:** Thought.

Hall Matters: Intelligence, wisdom, co-operative ventures, compatabilities, ecological concerns, friends and enemies, politics.

Need: Tribality.

Attribute: Co-operative.   **Weakness:** Pessimism.

Rune Rede for Mannaz:

Shining Stave - Upright or Unobstructed:

You now know yourself to be immortal essence. Discipline of the desires/needs of the mortal body through honed intelligence has produced a balanced personality - a nobility of spirit. You know where humanity's conflicts originate - to differentiate between want and need. Your understanding of the human condition, through self-analysis, has stimulated a patient approach to the life journey. Cultivate your critical faculties to maximise your choices of action. This gift gives unlimited access to occult (hidden) reality. Use it to empower yourself and alleviate human suffering by waking others to

168

this truth. Be assertive, as you no longer need to fear death nor will you allow others to manipulate or control you through fear of material loss or emotional deprivation. Through pragmatism, your needs and wants can now be fulfilled without undue attachment or aversion, by maintaining a balance between subjective and objective reality.

Shadow Stave - Reversed/Inverted or Obstructed:

You focus on your, ie. the body's, mortality and dwell on your limitations and weaknesses. Maybe you feel that time is "slipping through your fingers ". This generates a sense of hopelessness and can lead to an ignorance of spiritual values, a selfishness that breeds baseness in your character. This attitude causes delusions and personality disorders - the very same mentality that categorises the planet only as an "economic resource" and people as either "predators or victims". Do not waste your intelligence in cynicism which is really angry depression. You are presently cut off from your higher Self and act without perception of the consequences of your actions. Know that all realms of consciousness can be experienced whilst in the human form - you are more than the sum of your sensual cognition. If you are frustrated with your limited horizon then try pushing your mental boundaries by experimenting with alternate paradigms. Curb your impatience and activate your critical faculties. Self-analysis will create a more objective perspective to life, an acceptance that will allow choices of action you are presently unable to perceive.

Mannaz Key Words:

Shining Stave: Embodied awareness, balanced personality, intelligence, memory, rational consciousness and mind, perception, knowledge of potential and limitations, truth of existence, self-control, nobility of spirit, humankind, social attitudes, legal matters, initiate, seeker, occult power.

Shadow Stave: Over-emphasis on mortality, dwelling on limitations, weakness, ignorance, rejection of spiritual values, depression, hopelessness, baseness, social disorientation, misuse of potential, self-delusion, fantasy, personality disorders, thoughtlessness, lying.

Rune 21

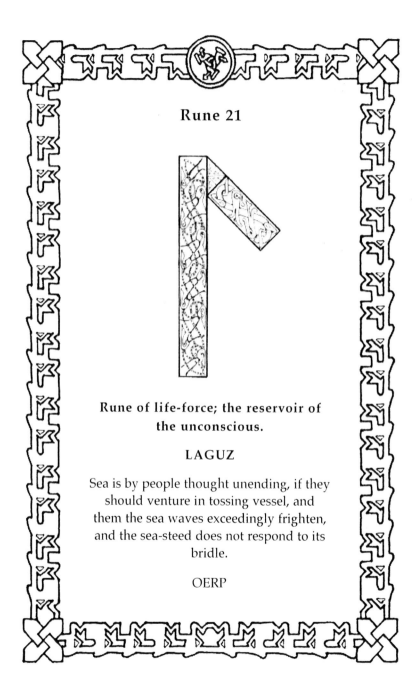

Rune of life-force; the reservoir of the unconscious.

LAGUZ

Sea is by people thought unending, if they should venture in tossing vessel, and them the sea waves exceedingly frighten, and the sea-steed does not respond to its bridle.

OERP

ᚺ (Laguz): Rune of Ferment and Fortitude.

Sound Value: l.   (pronounced "Larg-ooz")

Rune order sequence: No. 21.

Literal meaning: Lake, a body of water. Leek (herb).

Esoteric meaning: The ever present source of hidden vital energy; Magickal power.

Magickal meaning: "Conducting the Life-Force to Manifest Your Will".

Divinatory Meaning: Agitation of Emotions and Imagination.

Keywords: Vessel of vitality; Desire / Aversion.

Colour: Rainbow.   **Tree:** Osier.

Herb: Leek.   **Element:** Water.

Associated Diety: The Goddess Ran - "Plunder".

She is known as 'Mother of the Waves'. She is wife of the god Aegir (sea), who brews the god's ale drank in Asgard, and is held responsible for the drowning (called 'Ran's embrace') of people during storms at sea. She has nine daughters (waves) who cause distress to unwary ships enabling Ran to casts her 'golden net' over sailors, dragging them down to her domain.

It is with this net from which none escape, borrowed from Ran with the promise, which he did not keep of sharing the loot, that the mischievous Loki caught the dwarf Andvari (Careful-One) disguised in the shape of a salmon. Andvari had a secret hord of gold and precious objects stolen from the votive (sacrificial offering) areas in the river Rhine. Andvari handed over the trove with a curse that all who possessed any part of it would become insane with greed. Loki's stealing of Andvari's horde was to buy the freedom of the gods Odhinn (inspirer) and Hoenir (self?) who had been captured and held for ransom by the magician Hreidmar (frightener?) father of the shape-shifter Otr (otter) whom Loki had mistaken for an animal and slain for his beautiful hide. Otr was brother to Fafnir (embracer) who became a dragon when he in turn came into possession of Andvari's horde.

Her Hall is the reservoir of untapped and repressed lifeforce. Her Fetch animal (familiar) is the Sea Snake.

Dwelling Hall: Hlesey - "Sea Island".

Hall Colour: Rainbow.   **Hall Symbol:** The Sea Snake.

Hall Element: Water.   **Dominant Faculty:** Intuition.

Hall Matters: Emotion, Affection, sexuality, love, health, resources, hidden motivations, challengers, long journeys.

Need: Assurance.

Attribute: Stamina.   **Weakness:** Insecurity.

Rune Rede for Laguz:

Shining Stave - Upright or Unobstructed:

You are overcoming your fear of the life-journey through recognition of re-occurring patterns in your life, particularly by awareness of your emotional reactions that have caused you and others distress. You are allowing suppressed and/or repressed pain to surface and thus gain psychological insight into their source. You now know that the locking up of true emotional response such as grief, anger, sadness and even happiness lowers your available store of energy. This energy is always regenerative as its origin is in the make-up of the universal vitality. You can now not only heal yourself but become a vehicle for this vitality to express itself through creative thought, word and deed, thus gaining fertility of mind and body, which is its natural function. A time of transition and testing - go with the flow. Trust your intuition if dealing with others instability.

Shadow Stave - Reversed/Inverted or Obstructed:

You are in for a challenging period. The discipline of insight is needed to channel the tide of instability that you feel is quickly overtaking you. Over sensitivity can be the result of too much of your psyche being immersed in "undealt with" problems. These consume too much of your emotional energy thus leaving you with no reserve to swim with the current of your wyrd. Do not allow illusionary perceptions to breed fear and panic. You have unlimited power at your disposal (the universal sea of vitality from which all life is nourished) to generate the will and face the situations that are disturbing you. Withdrawal from the tests , ie. not dealing with them here and now, can result in ill health, physical and mental (one affects the other) and can result in a withering of your life-force and character.

Laguz Key Words:

Shining Stave: Life journey, recognition of patterns, psychological insight, the unconscious mind, surfaced problems, the sea of preconscious knowledge, hidden realms, flow of power, the sea of energy that separates life and death, stern tests, hidden resources, growth through integration, Masculine - phallic power, manly virtue, physical prowess, Feminine - imagination, emotion, psychic matters. Perception of primal law (orlog) in your life.

Shadow Stave: Lack of insight and direction, loss of stability, repetition of life lessons - "going around in circles", illusion, deception, over-sensitivity, emotional/psychological problems, ill-health, self - generated disease, inability to cope - "going under", avoidance, withdrawal, withering, psychic disturbance. Blockage of magickal power and strength of will.

Rune 22

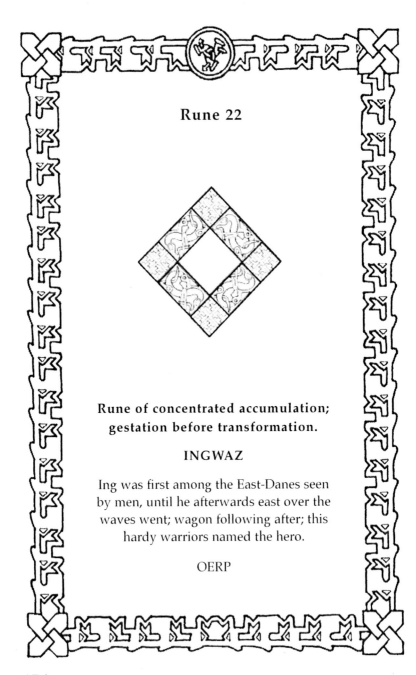

Rune of concentrated accumulation; gestation before transformation.

INGWAZ

Ing was first among the East-Danes seen by men, until he afterwards east over the waves went; wagon following after; this hardy warriors named the hero.

OERP

◊ (Ingwaz): Rune of Cohesion and Concentration.

Sound Value: ng (as in 'singer').

(pronounced "Eeng-varz")

Rune order sequence: No. 22.

Literal meaning: The Hero/God Ing; 'Son of (Njord)'; Beacon.

Esoteric meaning: Withdrawal from the world, after action, to facilitate the process of change into a higher state of being.

Magickal meaning: "Concentration of Accumulated Power for Future Manifestation".

Divinatory Meaning: Inactivity before or after Peak Experiences.

Keywords: Seed, Preparation, Gestation.

Colour: Silver.   **Tree:** Hazel.

Herb: Self-Heal.   **Element:** Salt.

Associated Diety: The God Freyr - the "Lord".

Son of Njord, twin brother of Freyja. He is of the race of gods called Vanir. He is a fertility god and is called upon for frith (fruitful peace at home) and is often pictured with an enlarged phallus. He is also a deity of love and pleasure. He is also a warrior-god and is called upon for protection in battle. He is seen as a giver of riches, and growth in all fields of endeavour. He is Lord of the Elves and is especially connected with the worship given to ancestral spirits and the spirits of nature.

Under the name Ing, he mysteriously appeared, from the west, in the land of the Angles (who later became part of the race known as the English) in Denmark. He brought peace,

177

harmony and plenty to the land. He sired a line of rulers and then just as mysteriously disappeared. Ing-Freyr personifies the male principle of immortality through rebirth.

He incurred Odhinn's wrath by mounting that god's High Seat which gave a view of all the Nine Worlds. While seated there, Freyr spied and fell in love with the rock-giantess Gerd (fenced-in). He send his sword and horse, as wooing gifts, with his servant Skirnir (bright-one) to Gerd. She rejected his marriage proposal. Freyr would not take 'no' for an answer. She later gave in after he threatened her with a runic curse of uncontrollable and unfulfillable sexual lust. He then waited in anguish for nine nights and days until she finally arrived.

His Hall is the home of the Light Elves, beings of thought and desire that determine form and function in nature. His Fetch animal (familiar), a counterpart to Freyja's sow, is the Boar called Gullinborsti (golden-bristles).

Dwelling Hall: Álfheim -   "Elf Home".

Hall Colour: Gold.   **Hall Symbol:** The Boar.

Hall Element: Air.   **Dominant Faculty:** Thought.

Hall Matters: Fertility, germination, hereditary, progeny, fatherhood, male mysteries, transistions, reincarnation, resources, responsibilities.

Need: Peace.

Attribute: Idealistic.   **Weakness:** Noncommital.

Rune Rede for Ingwaz:

Shining Stave - Upright or Unobstructed:

All beings need a period of withdrawal for regeneration. Self replenishment allows potential energy to release itself in its own time. A necessary measure of isolation before you start the

178

next phase of life. Not a state of indolence but submersion into your psycho-soul complex. It may be that you need to abandon a situation that is running down your reserves, on any level. You may have outgrown relationships or lifestyles that are non-supportive of your present maturity. For some men, preparation for fatherhood or great responsibility in society. This is the rune of preparation for 'rebirth', either as a radical change of direction in this life or putting your life in order before completion of the present cycle. Draw on all resources available to achieve confidence and clarity. Metaphysically it signifies the state of alertness between the conditions we call life and death, where the advanced soul retains its identity and consciously awaits rebirth back into the tribe to continue its development. In life you are now gathering your potential to soar ahead with the guarantee of success through correct preparation.

Shadow Stave - Reversed/Inverted or Obstructed:

Self-absorption without reflection leads to disassociation from objective reality and repetitious activity without evolution. Subjective emotions are the measure of your existence - these make you vulnerable to exploitation. You put off facing your tasks in this life by trying to stay in a childhood state of dependence on 'Authority constructs', eg. God, the State, whom you make responsible for your life. Do not be paralysed by the fantasy that your wyrd is fixed and unalterable. Unregenerate behaviour and habits leave you exhausted. If you are "sick and tired" of the demands of life, take a vacation and transform yourself by detoxification - sauna, spa, massage, diet, exercise and rest. If you are nearing the completion of your life passage through illness or old age, now is the time to prepare for separation from the body by deep reflection on your life to achieve peace. In life, you must accept responsibility for your own future and happiness by integrating all your knowledge to maximise your potential.

Ingwaz Key Words:

Shining Stave: Stored power, magickal reserve, ritual place, centreing of energy, meditation, release of energy (from potential to actual), self-replenishment, gestation, resting, expectations, internal growth (towards maturity), passive waiting for right moment to act, male fertility, impregnation, progeny, hereditary, nurturing, conscious withdrawal from situation, the fecundity of nature.

Shadow Stave: Self-absorption, disassociation from objective reality, subjective reactions, dissipation of energy, wasted emotion, repetitious activity without evolution, do not learn by mistakes, avoidance of maturation, wasting of potential, impotence, vulnerability, unregenerate, cut off from natural cycles of life.

Rune 23

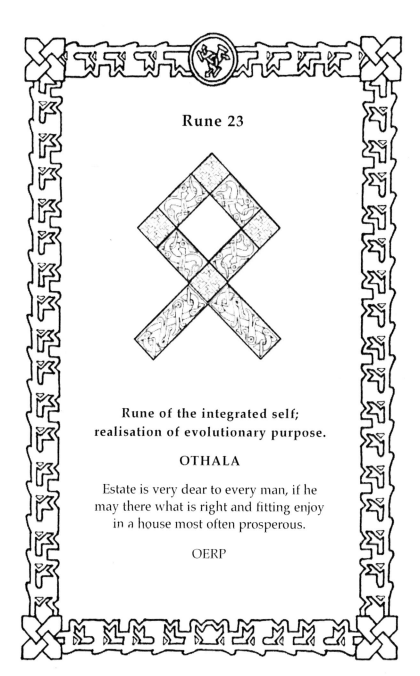

**Rune of the integrated self;
realisation of evolutionary purpose.**

OTHALA

Estate is very dear to every man, if he
may there what is right and fitting enjoy
in a house most often prosperous.

OERP

◊ (Othala): Rune of Rights and Reclamation.

Sound Value: o.   (pronounced "Oath-arl-ah")

Rune order sequence: No. 23.

Literal meaning: Noble; Ancestral Land (estate).

Esoteric meaning: The hereditary state of the Self both physical and spiritual.

Magickal meaning: "Accessing Power from the Individual and Collective Folk-Conscious".

Divinatory Meaning: Inheritance and Birth-right.

Keywords: Sacred Enclosure; Self.

Colour: Green.   **Tree:** Hawthorn.

Herb: Clover.   **Element:** Earth.

Associated Diety: The Goddess Saga - "History".

The Goddess of time and events, recall and memory. She is the patron of writers and story-tellers. She is one of the æsir goddesses - *Asynjur* (ON), the daughter of Odhinn and Frigga. It is suggested that she may be an aspect of Frigga in her capacity as "silent seeress" who 'dips into Urd's Well' for knowledge of the patterns of Wyrd. Saga sings the songs and chants the ancestral stories in the company of Odhinn. They drink together everyday from golden cups.

Ritual drinking was a sacred rite called a Symbel (or Sumbel). Its function was to gain inspiration and to honour the ancestors and deities through spontaneous recitation of praise poetry either newly conceived or passed down. This poetry was usually recited in an alliterative style not only for

182

particular emphasis but to enhance its ease of recall by those who heard it. The Symbol was also the place where individuals bound themselves to oaths of deeds (boasts) which had to be fulfiled even unto death and beyond.

Her Hall is the storehouse of all memory/reflection ie. the physical hereditary and racial memory necessity for the continuity of existence of the folk-collective - the tribe, and reawakening of the individual soul within its familiar framework. Her Fetch animal (familiar) is the Salmon.

Dwelling Hall: Sokkvabekk -   "Sunken Bench".

Hall Colour: Rainbow.   **Hall Symbol:** The Salmon.

Hall Element: Water.   **Dominant Faculty:** Intuition.

Hall Matters: Rights, spiritual service, mysticism, memories, secrets. Dwellings, property, domesticity, relatives, society.

Need: Privacy.

Attribute: Noble.   **Weakness:** Self-undoing.

Rune Rede for Othala:

Shining Stave - Upright or Unobstructed:

You have achieved a state of well being. This has come about by the balance of security and personal freedom. Knowing your place in the order of things allows self fulfilment and stability. You have claimed power and knowledge from past generations. This can be material as in property, wealth and other legacies and/or intellect, education and spiritual/occult wisdom. Through the use of custom and thew (connections that give mutual support), new ventures will be successful. New allegiances can generate mutual profit. Authorities and Institutions may look upon you with favour. You now have time to reflect on the results of right thought and action. Honour your forebears for your inheritance, whatever it may be and contemplate what contributions you are leaving for your family/society. Review your life up to date.

Shadow Stave - Reversed/Inverted or Obstructed:

You may find yourself without the support of family, clan or authority figures and/or without wealth or a home. You may be the victim of prejudice and/or suffer restrictions on personal liberty. You must realise that no one can take away from you your most important possession - your Self-will. We are the product of our ancestors' activities. It is for us to understand that the disruption of joyful tradition and customs, the under-mining of worthy authorities to the group detriment results in suffering for all. If you are suffering from the result of family and/or state corruption then seek the company and support of your natural "kinsmen" be they blood or adopted. Contribute for the gain of all. If you are corrupt yourself, then you will be tempted to misuse your power for selfish ends without regard to the long term consequences of your actions. You may find yourself bewailing your fate in another life. Take a good look at your life - how will you be remembered after your death?

Othala Key Words:

Shining Stave: Ritual enclosure, sacred site, inherited power and knowledge from past generations, boundaries (lawful), ties of blood, family and clans, mutual property, custom and order, inheritance, wealth, possessions (immobile), preserved freedom, stability with growth, new dwellings, new allegiances, established power ,authority, productive ventures, psychological boundaries of self, maintaining individuality, reflection on life's experiences, financial dynasties.

Shadow Stave: Disruption of tradition or customs, undermining of leaders or authority to group detriment, misuse of power, restriction of personal liberty, totalitarianism, cultural and racial prejudice, outlawry, desecration of sacred sites, homelessness, poverty, slavery.

Rune 24

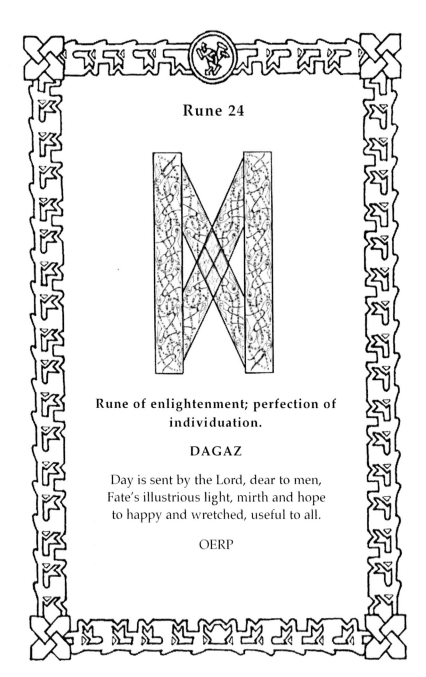

Rune of enlightenment; perfection of individuation.

DAGAZ

Day is sent by the Lord, dear to men,
Fate's illustrious light, mirth and hope
to happy and wretched, useful to all.

OERP

ᛞ (Dagaz): Rune of Reconciliation and Realisation.

Sound Value: d.   (pronounced "Darg-arz")

Rune order sequence: No. 24.

Literal meaning: Day (light of).

Esoteric meaning: Synthesis through the transcendence of polarities.

Magickal meaning: "Transcendence of Individual and Collective Definition".

Divinatory Meaning: Welfare through Cessation of Opposition.

Keywords: Synthesis; Syncronicity.

Colour: Indigo.   **Tree:** Spruce.

Herb: Clary.   **Element:** Iron.

Associated Diety: The God Forsetti - the "Reconciler of Deeds".

The God of law-giving, settler of law suits and quarrels. Patron god of the Frisians (the Germanic people who inhabited the Netherlands/Holland). Son of Baldur (bold) and his wife Nanna (mamma?), he is one of the Æsir. His hall is on an island, (on which no animal can be harmed), pillared with red gold and thatched with silver. It has a sacred spring brought forth from a rock with a blow from a double headed axe. Its waters, if drunk, give silent wisdom from the Well of Urd (that which is) which feeds the roots of Yggdrasil - the World Tree. The West Saxons called it Irminsul (primal pillar).

All the Nine Worlds lie within the span of the World Tree which is said to be an evergreen. At its roots gnaw the dragon Niddhogg (vicious blow) and many snakes; an eagle nests at its crown with a falcon between his eyes, and the squirrel Ratatosk runs up and down between them exchanging taunts. Four stags also gnaw on the World Tree's bark; but the Norn's sprinkling of the watersfrom the Well of Urdhr heal it each day.

His Hall is the place of peace that comes through the reconciliation of the unconscious with the superconscious, where the struggle between animal nature and god nature is finally transcended. This can be both the state of self-realisation /judgement in death or the state of cosmic enlightenment achieved in life - the reconciliation within the self of the opposing forces of order and chaos. His animal Fetch (familiar) is the Stork.

Dwelling Hall: Glitnir -   "Glistening".

Hall Colour: Red-gold.   **Hall Symbol:** The Stork.

Hall Element: Air.   **Dominant Faculty:** Thought.

Hall Matters: Spirituality, religion, occult, unions, contracts, lawsuits, public dealings, communal interests.

Need: Harmony.

Attribute: Fair.   **Weakness:**Ungrateful.

Rune Rede for Dagaz:

Shining Stave - Upright or Unobstructed:

You are experiencing a sudden awakening. You should be feeling a sense of tranquil wholeness. Through observation and inspiration you have perceived the mystery of Syncronicity - that things/events are connected and that seeming polar opposites can be reconciled. This is done when you accept that causality is not a linear projection of past, present, future but an infinite cyclic pattern of interacting forces connecting all the universe of mind, matter and spirit, rather like a spider's web. In Rune-lore, this is called The Web of Wyrd. Where ever you perceive yourself to be in this web, know that you have reached a primary understanding and that you have reason to hope that you will learn from your experiences. Old cycles have finished and new ones are about to begin. This is the rune of Ragnarok (destruction of the powers). How you use this knowledge will determine your personal power through the next cycle of your life.

Shadow Stave - Reversed/Inverted or Obstructed:

Your lack of insight into the patterns of causality known as The Web of Wyrd (that which is and is becoming) are causing irresolute behaviour. This can lead to ironic surprises and non-resolution of conflict in ideas and situations. You feel torn between extremes of thought and action, not knowing which is the right way to go. The more you try to set an "either/or" frame work to your situation, the more confusion results. A too analytical approach is not in your best interests. Know that you are both the cause and the result of your life-experiences. Do not blame others. Review your goals. You can overcome your feelings of hopelessness by accepting yourself as you are right now without self pity. This is the rune of Ragnarok (destruction of the powers). It is an opportunity for new beginnings. Adjustment to the reality of daily existence is an act of wisdom and will generate a sense of peace.

Dagaz Key Words:

Shining Stave: Transcendent awareness, sudden awakening, the eternal moment, resolution of duality and conflicts, mystical insight and inspiration, initiation, cosmic consciousness, transmission, polar exchange, completion, reason for hope, joy, happiness, triumph, new beginnings, synchronistic opportunity, sudden understanding, transformation, the ideal, totality.

Shadow Stave: Missed opportunity, sudden reversals, lack of insight, non-resolution of conflicts (ideas or situations), irresolute behaviour, ironic situations, lack of goals, incompletion, ennui, boredom, dullness and hopelessness.

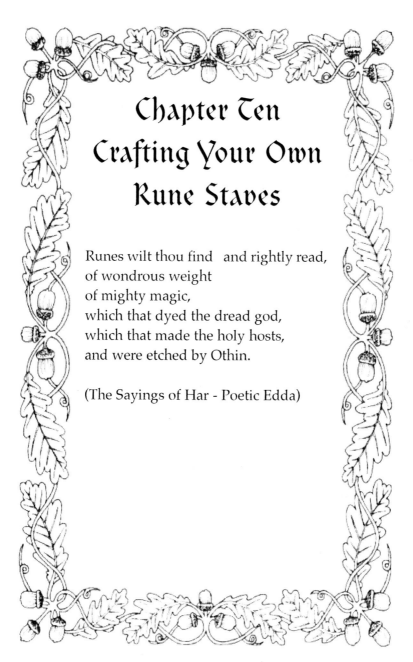

Chapter Ten
Crafting Your Own
Rune Staves

Runes wilt thou find   and rightly read,
of wondrous weight
of mighty magic,
which that dyed the dread god,
which that made the holy hosts,
and were etched by Othin.

(The Sayings of Har - Poetic Edda)

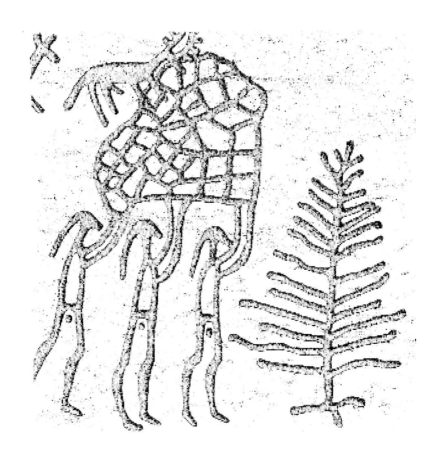

192

Chapter Ten
Crafting Your Own Runes

If you do not already have a set of runes, you may wish to craft your own. Wood and bone are suitable for a personal Futhark. Although runes can be scored on metal and stone or any object that has special significance for you. It is best to avoid synthetic materials. Painting or staining the runes on appropriate materials is also a choice.

Risting

Risting is the act of cutting or sawing especially used in relation to the runes. It comes from the Old Norse word *Rista*. If you decided to use wood, the most expedient way is to purchase dowelling from a hardware store. Select a timber for which you have an attraction. Remember that a seed-bearing tree, be it fruit, nut or cone, is the most traditional. Cut the length into 24 pieces with a thickness with which you feel comfortable.

For those who desire to partake in the ancient customs, it is appropriate for you to select a living tree for your timber source. Approach it with reverence, for it is a living being. Ask its spirit for permission to take a branch. The power of the tree will be in your Rune staves. If possible, choose a branch pointing north. When cutting, keep in your mind the purpose for which you are severing it. There are several methods you can use to make the blanks to receive the staves. With a sharp knife, hand axe or fret saw take slivers from the branch at a 45 degree angle; or split the branch into thin planks and them saw them into 24 pieces; or cut across the branch, the same as cutting dowel.

Whether you "finish" the 24 pieces ie. remove the bark and sand them down or leave them in their natural state is up to you to decide.

Now you are ready to rist or score the Runes on your staves. Prepare yourself psychologically and spiritually by quietening the mind. When you are ready, concentrate on the task before you. Contemplate Odhinn as the Rune Master. Chant an invocation that you have memorised that concentrates you intention and invokes your will to impart power to the risting; or recite the following example:

Woden Within

Woden Without

Help my Hand

To Rist the Runes Aright.

Drawing the rune shapes in pencil on your stave blanks before you begin risting is a sure way to ensure accuracy for the finished set. Always start from the bottom and work up and/or outwards. This can be difficult to master as we are used to drawing or cutting in the opposite direction. There is a magickal reason for this reversal. We are drawing the power of the runes from the natural elements, from the earth, so to remind the runer from whence he/she draws their power and to channel it magickally, we follow this method. It is important to make an effort to retain the traditional Runic proportions when preparing runes for divination and magickal usage. These proportions will give a volume area that is divisible by three, such as four units high by one and a half wide or four units high by three units wide. Working out the proportions for the rest of the runes yourself will give you a good feel of their structure. By observation of each stave before commencement of drawing or risting, you will find that no one rune has more than six component strokes.

194

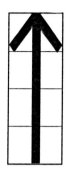 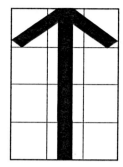

(Fig.1)

An example of runic proportion is illustrated above (see Fig.1).

Chanting

With a sharp knife (traditionally, one that has been set aside and dedicated specifically for this puropse) or wooden carving tool, commence to rist the runes one at a time in the Futhark order (ie. starting with Fehu and finishing with Othala). Think of each rune's meaning and chant its name to yourself as you work. It may not be possible to do all in one sitting. If this is the case, then only do one aett at a time, that is from Fehu to Wunjo, then Hagalaz to Sowilo and finally, Tiwaz to Othala. In magickal lore, the best time for risting is the waxing moon, that is, between the new and the full moon.

Staining and Claiming

The next stage is staining your runes. You may use pigment, ochre or paint. Red is the traditional colour as it represents the fiery force of creative energy. This is reflected in our own bodies in the colour of our blood, our own life force. When staining, you are claiming the runes as your own by symbolically adding your life force to them. To continue ancient tradition, you may choose to add your own blood to the pigment or just use your blood alone for the staining.

Prepare yourself as you did before risting the runes. In magickal lore, the optimum time to stain the runes would be the three nights of the full moon (one night for each aett or the middle night of the three for staining them all). Using a thin paintbrush or appropriate tool, paint in the grooves using single line strokes, much the same as you would if you were painting or drawing them on paper. You can tidy them up after the basic lines that compose the rune are stained in the grooves. Use the Futhark order. Whilst doing so think of each rune being alive with power; recite its name and/or qualities. When you have finished, chant a song of power of your own devising to fix your intent; or recite the following example:

Urd, Verdhandi, Skuld,

In Well and Web be Found

Rune Might flows by Cunning Skill

And in these Staves be Bound

Now spend some time in meditation on your completed ritual and its significance.

Place the completed rune stave set in a natural material bag eg. linen, wool or leather or a wooden, metal or stone box ready for use. If you don't need to use the rune's immediatley, it is traditional to wrap them in dark cloth and conceal them for a period of nine days. This is symbolic of gestation.

You can choose to do this or not. Concealing them for nine hours or even nine minutes still enacts the ritual significance of creation, gestation and birth. By doing so you are mythologically (and magickally) recognising the rune stave set as a living entity ie. a source of cognative awareness, that you have brought into being. This ritual engenders respect for the runic mysteries and the handling of your staves.

The staining of the runes can be done to your store-bought set, whether they are new or you have had them for some time. By painting (or applying your own blood) in the grooves, you are recharging and personalising the runic vitality inherent in the Rune shapes.

The use of Linseed oil as a preservative for wooden rune staves is traditional. This oil will prevent the paint/pigment or blood from being worn away from constant handling. It also stops wood from splitting as it tends to dry out and loose its own natural oils over time. Some runers choose to use a natural varnish such as Shellac to finish and seal their staves. This can also be used on stone and its compounds such as fired clay.

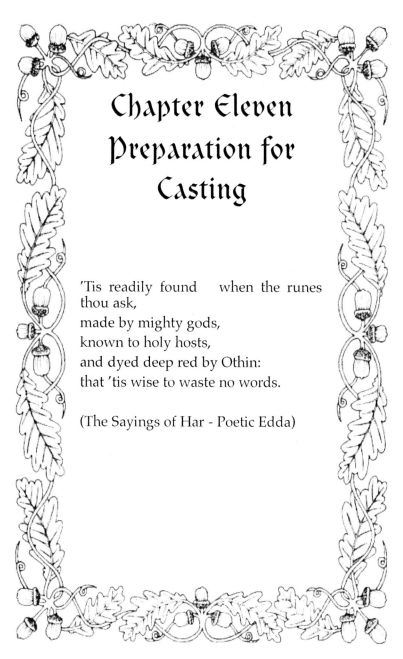

Chapter Eleven
Preparation for Casting

'Tis readily found   when the runes
thou ask,
made by mighty gods,
known to holy hosts,
and dyed deep red by Othin:
that 'tis wise to waste no words.

(The Sayings of Har - Poetic Edda)

Chapter Eleven
Preparation for Casting

The basis of all meanings in rune layouts have to be related to the concept of the two-fold division of time with the allowance of what is yet to come. To each division was assigned a female deity who was not only a guardian of her division but also a living expression of its function. These beings are known as the great "Norns". Their relationship is:

Urd: that which has become - the immutable past, which has objective reality.

Verdhandi: that which is becoming - the fluctuating present, which has subjective reality.

Skuld: that which should be (coming) - the unmanifested present (future), which is dependent on the interplay of the two other functions.

Before attempting any casting, the Runer should prepare him/herself psychologically and spiritually. This is best done by firstly seating themselves, facing North (the sacred ancestral direction) if possible, then breathing deeply and rhythmically emptying the mind and relaxing the body.

When extraneous thoughts have quieted down, contemplate the Three Norns (Nornir) and their functions. Tune yourself to the vibrations of the Web of Wyrd. Know that the only realities are the ever-present "past" and the ever-changing "now". The "future" is only a potentiality. You can call on the Norns either mentally or out loud. Chant *Urd, Verdhandi, Skuld* until you sense an attunement with the patterns of time. Next call on Odhinn, as Master of Rune Lore, for the inner vision to read the runes correctly, with this simple formula or something similar:

Woden within

Woden without

Open my Eye

To Read the Runes Aright

You will feel when the time is right to begin your casting.

In all methods, it is advisable to lay out a white cloth as a neutral field to cast or place your runes. This is traditional and serves not only to keep your runes clean, but provides a psychic field free from distraction when you are contemplating their meaning, regardless whether you are selecting the runes to place in a pre-ordained pattern or casting them at random. In some forms of casting, a grid for working, composed of three concentric circles representing from inner to outer - Urd, Verdhandi, Skuld - is either marked on it or is super-imposed mentally.

When formulating the question, hold the rune bag (or lot container) in your hands. If you are asking for someone who is present you may allow them to hold the bag before you do, to assist in attuning the runes. It is important that the querent have a clear cut question. The runes reveal their meanings best if approached precisely. Thus you should avoid framing ambiguous queries until you develop the skill to read on multiple levels. When casting for someone else, have them speak the question. This focuses their thoughts. It also helps you to choose your level of interpretation, ie. material, emotional, mental or spiritual, or a blend of any.

As your intuitional/psychic skills develop, coupled with your knowledge, you may discover that verbalisation of the question by the inquirer is not always needed. You may find yourself getting "flashes" of meaning or mental pictures and words, but do not be afraid to ask questions. Sometimes a key word on their behalf will help unlock deeper meaning.

If you are unsure of an interpretation, review the elements that stand out. They will usually "latch on" to you. In psychic matters, it is best not to over-analyse or be too logical. Remember, the conscious mind is a receiver of the hidden (unconscious) knowledge and is not the sole arbiter in your decisions. Feel what is right rather than think it. If you feel you cannot understand what the runes are telling you, try another spread. Reword the question. Approach it from another direction.

Consulting the rune rede in this book, on a regular basis will eventually lay down the intellectual foundation for you to be able to work spontaneously with your own interpretations of individual castings. Always remember to record your castings, so you may come back to them at a later date for reference.

By doing this, you may consciously observe the Web of Wyrd in action. It also will reveal to you how your divination ability is progressing - your perception of the Orlog in the Well. Treat the runes with respect. It is not advisable to let others handle your staves unless it is part of your method for rede giving.

By handling the runes exclusively, you intermingle your psychic field with them, establishing a strong resonance. If your friends wish to experiment or learn rune casting, have a spare set allocated for general use.

When you have finished your reading, you may close the procedure by chanting affirming words of thanks such as:

Hail the Norns that Nurture All!

Hail the Well that Wards All!

Hail the Rede that Rights All!

204

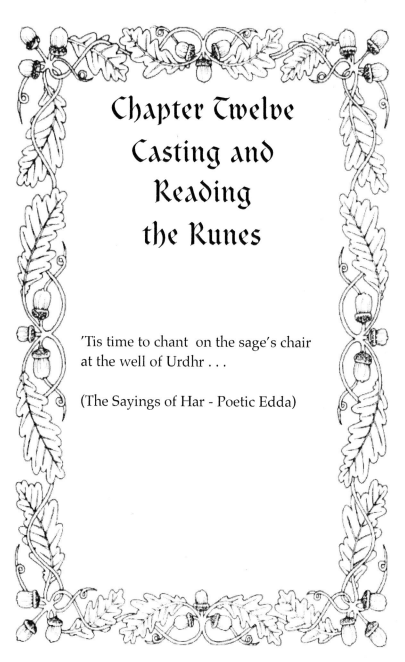

Chapter Twelve
Casting and
Reading
the Runes

'Tis time to chant on the sage's chair
at the well of Urdhr . . .

(The Sayings of Har - Poetic Edda)

Chapter Twelve
Casting and Reading the Runes

In this chapter, some basic casting methods are given. They are quickly learned, their simplicity freeing the runer from having to memorise complicated layouts at an early stage.

A 'shining' rune stave is one in its original upright position and unobstructed - not partially nor wholly covered. An 'shadow' rune stave is one which is either inverted (upside down), reversed or obstructed by another stave - partially or wholly covered. This applies to all casting methods. By observation you will see that there are nine runes that are non-invertible. These are Gebo (X), Hagalaz (N), Nauthiz (⟩), Isa (|), Jera (⟩), Eihwaz (∫), Sowilo (⟩), Ingwaz (◇), Dagaz (M). Five runes out of this nine which are non-reversible - Hagalz, Nauthiz, Jera, Eihwaz and Sowilo. There are also four runes out of this nine that do not change appearance no matter if they are reversed or inverted - Gebo, Isa, Ingwaz and Dagaz.

Rune Combinations

There are a possible 576 rune combinations from 24x24. If you also take into account the three levels of interpretation based on the three Aetts - 3x576 - then you get 1728 rune combinations (which adds up to 18 = 9 (N), the Mother Rune)! The mathematicians among you might wish to works out even more combinations but this aspect starts to overlap into magickal study especially if the numerological aspects of the runes are taken into consideration. Suffice to say, in time, by observing/recording your rune castings you will notice certain combinations that affirm the overall message of the Rede and/or confirm the meaning of certain surrounding runes.

I have found that the runes Gebo, Isa, Ingwaz and Dagaz being constant, in that their shape cannot be distorted, can act as poles or as an axis for other runes to group around. Their power never wavers so they can override surrounding shinning or shadow staves or alternatively consolidate the surrounding patterns. Two other runes also act in this function - Ehwaz and Mannaz which are symmetrical staves. Though not constant and invertible, they are non-reversible. In their upright position they act as amplifiers/transmitters of the runes energy before, after, underneath or over them. In the inverted position they as "circuit breakers" to the same energy thus weakening and/or isolating their influence. These same principles can be applied to their magickal applications.

It will enhance your understanding of the Rede given in the following layouts if you make note of which Aett they come from. By cross referencing with the numerological information given in the chapter six; The Runic Code, you may find a particular pattern or focus. If you come by an accumulation of rune staves from a particular Aett, this will suggest that this is an area of importance for you to investigate and to contemplate further. So for easy reference the three-fold sequence is repeated:

Freyja's Eight: The awakening of 'The Self': The individual and collective social journey in the world - understanding Orlog - "That which has become".

Hagal's Eight: The testing of 'The Self': The individual and collective psychological journey - experiencing Wyrd- "That which is becoming".

Tyr's Eight: The actualising of the 'The Self': individual and collective spiritual journey - intuiting Skuld - "That which shall (is obliged to) come".

A One Stave Method

This method is invaluable when seeking a simple Yes or No to a question. Select a rune at random. A Shinning Stave is *Yes*, a Shadow Stave is *No*. A less shallow way of dealing with the one stave layout involves contemplating the message given by the rune.

A Two Stave Method

When taken in advance of a situation, it can guide your behaviour or attitude. Try selecting a stave each morning before you begin your daily routine. As the day progresses, reflect on events. See if you can relate them to your interpretation of the rune. Alternatively, you can just passively relate circumstances to the rune and contemplate them at the end of the day. This is an excellent way to attune yourself to the subtleties of Rune Lore.

This can also be done in reverse by selecting a random rune at the end of the day to explore a situation you wish to understand more clearly.

Example (Fig.1): A person draws the rune of Fehu in the morning before shopping. This indicates to them the circulation of money. This seems ambiguous! During the excursion, they pass a lottery office and remembering Fehu, they buy an instant lottery ticket and win a small amount of money.

On going home, they draw another stave. This time the rune is Wunjo (inverted). This is interpreted as unhappiness or discontent at not achieving their wish for a big win.

(Fig.1)

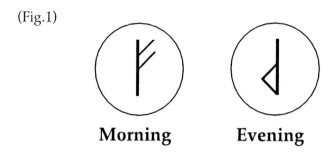

Morning   Evening

The Well Of Wyrd - A Three Stave Layout

This method can be approached in two ways. The traditional method is to cast all the runes on the white cloth. With eyes closed, select three staves at random.

The second way is to stir the runes in your bag until one seems to stick to your fingers. Repeat the process until three staves have been withdrawn.

Place them as illustrated below (Fig.2). If the blank side is facing up, turn the staves over from left to right as if you were turning the pages of a book. This keeps them in their original "landing" position. Contemplate the interplay of energies remembering that:

Position One represents the causes, actions and thoughts that are at the foundation of the question or problem.

Position Two is what is happening now, the ever-changing present . . . your situation and your attitudes.

Position Three indicates the probable outcome, that which should come into manifestation, dependent on the intermingled influences from Positions One and Two.

If a simple Yes or No answer is required, the outcome can be judged by the tally of staves in positive and obstructed positions in the layout.

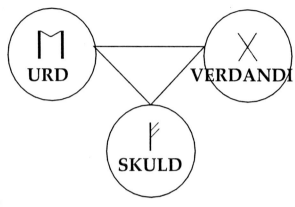

(Fig.2)

If all three are shining, the answer is *Yes*. If all are shadow, *No*. If two are shadow or two shining, focus on the rune in the position of Skuld, the outcome.

If it is shining, *Yes* is still your answer. If shadow, take it as *No*. In these circumstances, it is best to examine the layout to understand the interplay of energies.

The Nornic method works best when information is required to make a decision. Such as:

"Should I enter into this new business venture?"

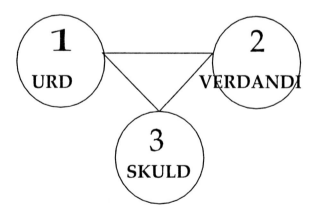

Reading

Ehwaz in the Urd position - This Shinning Stave indicates the querist has a strong ability to work closely with others. He has the capacity to win trust and inspire loyalty. Swift progression is also indicated. This puts him in a good position.

Gebo in the Verdhandi position - This Shinning Stave indicates reciprocity with his potential business partners, but he should draw up binding contracts and ensure that all agree with the arrangements.

Fehu in the Skuld position - This Shinning Stave indicates new beginnings and an increase in financial prosperity and personal power.

Based on this layout, the venture should be successful as long as the querist covers himself with legal contracts. Gebo is one of the non-invertible runes: in any position, it looks the same. In this case, the reader must take pains to "feel out" the stave in relation to the other runes. If in doubt, consider the positive aspects as an emphasis to avoid the obstructive qualities. As a general rule, inverted runes and reversed runes are considered obstructive. The runer will quickly become familiar with the non-invertible and non-reversible runes by scanning the Futhark order or refering to the beginning of this chapter.

The Valknut - A Nine Stave Layout

This literally translates as the "knot of the slain" and esoterically as "bindings of the chosen". It represents the interplay of the energies of the nine worlds through the process of time. On the World tree (Yggdrasil), Odhinn perceived that events, including 'destiny', could be bound or unbound by his manipulation of the Runes. The Valknut is also called Valgrind - "gate of the slain or chosen", see chapter thirteen; Magickal Application of the Runes.)

211

The staves are chosen as in the Nornic Matrix but now the process is repeated two more times. Lay out the runes as illustrated (see Fig.3).

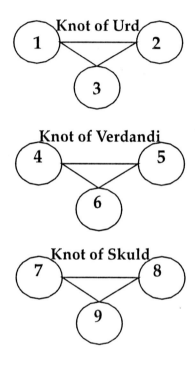

(Fig.3)

Urd's Knot represents the causes, actions and thoughts that are at the foundation of the question or problem.

Verdhandi's Knot is what is happening now, the ever changing present . . . your situation and your attitudes.

Skuld's Knot indicates the probable outcome, that which should come into manifestation, dependent on the intermingled influences from the previous knots.

212

When reading this method, remember to synthesise the basic Nornic progression - Urd, Verdhandi, Skuld - in each knot before going on to the next. The focus of the first knot, the number three position leads you into reading the second knot. The focus of the second knot, the number six position, leads into the third knot. The focus of the whole reading, if the final outcome is what you are seeking, is in the number nine position.

To enhance the interpretation of the whole Valknut, look at the relationship of the particular Norn in each separate knot in both the progressive and cumulative sequence:

1, 4, 7;

2, 5, 8;

3, 6, 9.

The following example (see Fig.4) like all readings given in this chapter was an actual consultation on a real situation. Like the Three-Rune Layout, it deals with a business arrangement and is a continuation of the last question. In this case, the querist returned for further Rede as he was unsure if the venture would work out because after the initial enthusiasm of the concerned parties, they still could not achieve cohesion nor agree on a collective direction. Much tarrying had occurred.

The question asked was: *"How do we regain cohesion to achieve our original goals"?*

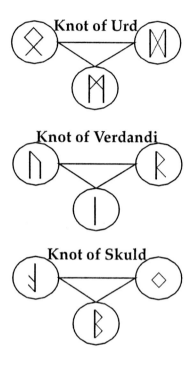

Knot of Urd

Knot of Verdandi

Knot of Skuld

(Fig.4)

Reading

Urd's Knot position one - Othala (upright) - This Shinning Stave indicates right order must be maintained, a leader should be designated for the group. Goals should be worked towards with mutual benefit in mind. A sharing of responsibility is needed. Flexible attitudes will avoid tension.

Urd's Knot position two - Dagaz (non-invertible) - This Shinning Stave indicates that you should channel all your ideas and skills towards your ideal. The use of insight is needed to balance your particular personalities. This will provide the incentive to begin.

Urd's Knot position three - Mannaz (upright) - This Shinning Stave indicates to use your intelligence. A structural scheme is needed and to which you should adhere. Each person's needs as well as limitations should be recognised. Work for a congenial environment. Maintain a happy disposition.

Verdhandi's Knot position four - Uruz (upright) - This Shinning Stave indicates you must have tenacity to succeed. Defend the group from inner collapse and failure by constant monitoring of the situation. Control enthusiasm by directing it towards your long-term goals. Pace yourself. General luck is indicated.

Verdhandi's Knot position five - Raidho (upright) - This Shinning Stave indicates a long hard passage ahead, with many periods where fatigue may weaken the resolve. Continued growth will occur but only through effort. Be prepared to take advice. Be rational when dealing with changing circumstances. Action should be undertaken only after planning. Be certain that your co-workers have respect for the product's origins.

Verdhandi's Knot position six - Isa (non-invertible) - This Shinning Stave is ambiguous, difficulties may arise in putting ideas into action. A period of stasis is indicated. Be careful you do not lose your influence. Beware of deceit or "rip-offs". Your original ideas are the basis of this venture. Even though your position may be weakened, you must not let your will slacken. Strive to maintain unity of purpose amongst the group.

Skuld's Knot position seven - Ansuz (inverted) - This Shadow Stave indicates to beware of delusions regarding the project. Poor judgement by yourself or others will lead to confusion. Beware of being manipulated. Discontent will arise. Make sure you know what is going on - a testing period.

Skuld's Knot position eight - Ingwaz (non-invertible) - This Shinning Stave is ambiguous, a conscious withdrawal from the

215

situation is indicated. This should be done to regather your energies. Let things rest for a while. When the time is right, you will act appropriately. A period of creativity and activity will follow as a result of new ideas.

Skuld's Knot position nine - Berkano (upright) - This Shinning Stave indicates a new start within the group. A continuation from the old, but with new aspects. These changes will be gradual at first, expanding towards new horizons. You will need to be crafty and self-contained to get your due. This is especially so when dealing with the designated leader. Prosperity will come if good business sense prevails.

The World Tree - A Nine Stave Method

This method uses the Nine Worlds as a model to build a holistic picture of yourself within the situation for which you are consulting the runes. Before using the layout, it is recommended that you become familiar with the cosmology as outlined in the chapter (2) on the Nine Worlds.

Lay your selected runes in the numerical order given below (see Fig.5). When contemplating their meaning it is important to maintain the sequential connection. When the connections have been made then observe the runes in their three particular designated groupings or tiers in this order - **[1, 5, 6] Midgard, the Realm of Action; then [2, 3, 4] Asgard, the Realm of Consciousness; then [7, 8, 9]. Niflheim, the Realm of Unconsciousness.**

Other combinations and connections between the tiers and individual worlds are obvious but to describe these would unnecessarily complicate the layout. I will leave them for the runer to explore.

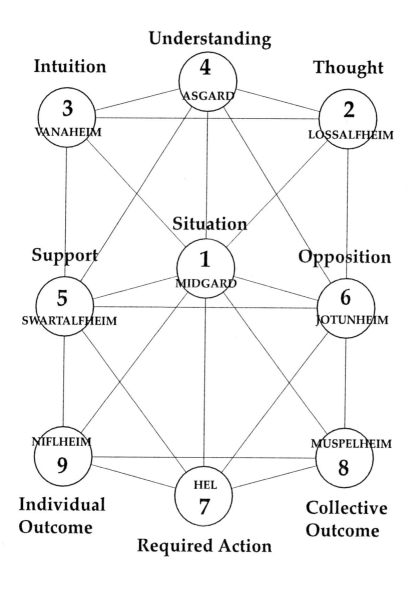

(Fig.5)

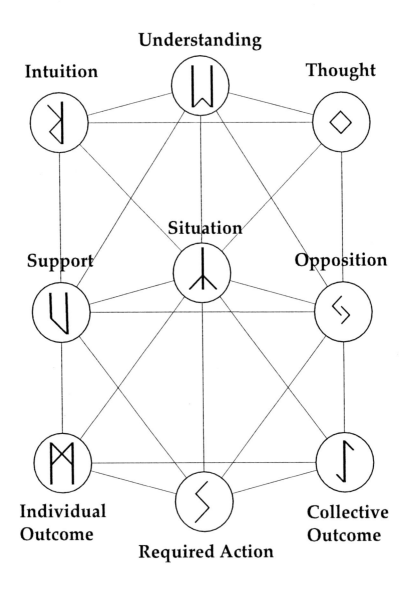

(Fig.6)

218

This layout (Fig.6) is not a simple question and answer format. Its function is to view the permutations of your present concern in a manner that gives guidance concerning the overall situation. The querist in this matter felt he was being made the scapegoat within a spiritual group, which he founded, because of his bluntness of speech in revealing what he saw as self seeking behaviour among a cliche. He wished to gain Rede on the degenerating situation. So the question asked was:

"What do I need to know and do to move beyond this conflict?"

Reading

Position one: Situation - Elhaz (inverted) - With this Shadow Stave, the querist is under attack and the group is losing its spiritual cohesiveness through the build up of negative psychological thoughts among themselves. Betrayal, loss of support and hidden dangers are indicated.

Position two: Thought - Ingwaz (non-invertible) - With this Shinning Stave, the querist is thinking that it would be best for him to withdrawal from the conflict as he has said his piece and done all he can do to for the group. Because of the shadow stave preceding, the querist is possibly feeling that it is all a waste of time and energy without a chance of getting better.

Position three: Intuition - Raidho (inverted) - With this Shadow Stave, the querist's intuition confirms to him that no further progress will be made with debate nor will appealing to group spiritual values and established resolution-of-conflict practices solve the situation.

Position Four: Understanding - Ehwaz (inverted) - With this Shadow Stave, the querist's understanding is that the conflicting parties can no longer hope to regain harmony. The mutual understanding, spiritual disciplines, goals and affection that once held them together have been replaced with enmity .

219

Position Five: Support - Uruz (inverted) - With this Shadow Stave, the querist sees that in this matter he has little support from within the group. In fact many see him as the aggressor and perhaps even a bully. It also indicates that he must stand his ground, alone if necessary, and actively defend himself against the clique whose actions are breaking up the structure of the group.

Position Six: Opposition - Jera (non-invertible) - This is a Shinning Stave but because of the shadow staves preceding, it indicates that opposition to a resolution has been actively building up over a period of time. Also that opposition to the querist is a result of actions and reactions by both parties in an earlier time, perhaps in the previous year. It is obvious that it will continue until reaching an apogee but it will finally end.

Position Seven: Required Action - **Sowilo (non-invertible)** - Because of the shadow nature of the previous rune staves, this Shining Stave warns the querist not to look to short-cuts nor hasty action in solving this problem. The obstacles for reconciliation are apparent and he can only continue to be truthful, maintain the original direction of the group until he has achieved the goals he has set both for himself and for the collective.

Position Eight: Collective Outcome - Eihwaz (non-invertible) - This Shining Stave continues with the ambiguous shadowy nature of the previous staves. The Rede is that endurance is needed during a time when it will appear that the group entity is finished in its present form but the spiritual message is that the experiences should be viewed as a form of personal initiation for all involved. Those who are flexible enough to explore the threads of what has happened will survive this psychological winter.

Position Nine: Individual Outcome - Mannaz - (upright) - This Shinning Stave suggests that the querist will be pragmatic about the situation knowing that all things must pass whether desired or undesired. Acceptance of this reality will enhance his spiritual state. There will be no loss of personal power but rather an increased understanding of the needed practicalities - to achieve a balance between individual and collective needs - when dealing with individuals in any society whether a small spiritual group or the larger community.

The Futhark - A 24-Rune Method

As its name indicates, this layout (see Fig. 7 & Fig. 8) is structured in the pattern of the three Aetts. The 24 steads representing fields of inquiry are determined by essential elements of the original rune stave meanings.

You may also choose to select one Aett at a time to get specific Rede in the area of your inquiry such as social concerns, psychological concerns or spiritual concerns. Alternatively you may seek Rede from each Aett or all collectively in terms or understanding Orlog, understanding Wyrd and/or understanding Skuld. Remember that no one Aett or individual stead is insulated from the other - all have elements of the social, psychological and spiritual intertwined. You may choose to accept the positions 8, 16 and 24 as summations of each separate Aett but it is important to remember in this method that each rune stave describes the condition of each stead in the present.

If you wish to use this method as a 'Life' Reading and read the runes sequentially and/or numerologically you may do so. It is important to note that this method is not a 'Life Passage' Prediction - it can only tell you where you are right now and what should manifest from the moment of rune casting.

1	2	3	4	5	6	7	8
Finances & Beginnings	Health & Vitality	Opposition & Reaction	Motivation & Inpiration	Advice & Action	Talents & Skills	Gifts & Obligations	Yearnings & Society
9	**10**	**11**	**12**	**13**	**14**	**15**	**16**
Crises & Changes	Restrictions *& Needs	Integrity & Isolation	Reward & Planning	Exploration & Endurance	Opportunity & Luck	Support & Protection	Guidance & Goals
17	**18**	**19**	**20**	**21**	**22**	**23**	**24**
Sacrifice & Acheivement	Continuity & Growth	Harmony & Discipline	Practicality & Co-operation	Emotions & Love	Completion & Analysis	Inheritance & Rights	Awareness & Evolution

(Fig.7)

The next chart (Fig.8) is an example of a reading done for each stead in the specific area of inquiry:

222

1	2	3	4	5	6	7	8
ᚼ	ᚱ	ᚦ	ᛚ	ᚠ	ᚺ	◇	ᛉ

9	10	11	12	13	14	15	16
ᛋ	ᛩ	ᚲ	ᛗ	ᚢ	ᚹ	↓	ᛗ

17	18	19	20	21	22	23	24
ᛁ	ᚨ	ᛋ	ᛏ	ᛤ	ᛁ	ᛒ	ᚷ

Fig.8)

Reading

Nauthiz in first field or stead shows the discontent through lack of money, indicating that the querist should be more self-reliant in this pursuit.

Raidho in the second stead shows an ordered program for healthier living is needed to maintain vitality.

Thurisaz in the third stead shows a state of reaction to the opposition he has encountered. As Thurisaz is the ruler of this stead, it is a justifiable feeling. The counsel is to control and focus this energy to change the situation for your benefit.

Eihwaz in the fourth stead shows that inspiration will come about by calling on inner resources. He has the power to deal with this situation.

223

Ansuz in the fifth stead shows that he should listen to divine guidance (Woden within) as well as use his intellectual abilities to get his life in order.

Hagalaz in the sixth stead shows that the present crisis, though seeming to negate his creative efforts, will actually force him into new areas of expression.

Ingwaz in the seventh stead shows that what appears as an end of a situation (following on from Hagalaz) is actually a needed rest. This gift is a time of regeneration and transformation before further action.

Elhaz in the eighth stead shows that the protection of the self is needed as he is under attack (refer back to the third stead). The way to deal with this is not to retaliate on the same level but to use his wisdom and craft.

Jera in the ninth stead shows that a cycle has been completed - prosperity and peace will come as a result of the changes, with a possible move to a new physical environment.

Othala in the tenth stead shows that discontent arises from the lack of right order and responsibility, with the group and society, with whom the querist identifies.

Kenaz in the Eleventh stead shows a constriction of creative ability and erotic energy. This is probably due to nervous tension generated by the feelings of self-doubt and failure.

Dagaz in the twelfth stead alerts the querist to be aware of seeming coincidences, eg chance meetings, that will be rewarding on the physical and/or spiritual levels.

Uruz (inverted) in the thirteenth stead shows a lack of consistency in directing his will. A lack of perspective generated through obsessive rigidity. Meditation is needed to balance the disharmony within.

224

Ehwaz (inverted) in the fourteenth stead shows a breakdown in the partnership. On the career side, it indicates mistrust and betrayal leading to separation. On the personal (romantic) side, it shows that the querist may be too demanding of his lover, to compensate for the lack in other life areas.

Tiwaz (inverted) in the fifteenth stead shows that the querist needs to overcome his paralysis of action. He has allowed himself to become confused through a sense of injustice. Strive to re-focus.

The last three steads show an obstructed group of energies. The help needed to rectify the distortion is shown in the next field.

Mannaz in the sixteenth stead shows that the guidance needed can be found by realisation of the querist's own potential. His talents and strengths are awaiting self activation. He must reset his goals and not give in to despair.

Laguz (inverted) in the seventeenth stead is again allied to the previous obstructed steads. It shows there is a fear of change which is causing the vital force to be dammed up. Courage is needed to regain self-mastery (see Mannaz in the previous position).

Fehu in the eighteenth stead shows that when a renewal is undertaken with a commitment to growth, then money will be forthcoming. Old ideas will be reworked to achieve success. Family support will rekindle the necessary drive.

Sowilo in the nineteenth stead indicates that career opportunities could lay in the area of counselling and teaching. Also, your lover/partners advice should be heeded in this matter.

Wunjo (inverted) in the twentieth stead shows the querist feels alienated within society. Loss of individuality within the group mind causes sorrow and a sense of disharmony.

Perthro in the twenty first stead shows that he gains pleasure from fellowship and the sharing of emotions. Challenges of growth led to fortunate opportunities for spiritual maturation.

Isa in the twenty second stead shows that he needs to unify his energies. Less dissipation and more self-control. Review his feelings of alienation and get rid of the illusions regarding his own ego.

Berkano in the twenty third stead shows that unexpected opportunity will arise to continue his past projects within the community, likely from ancestral inspiration or past life motivation. He will gain assistance to improve on them. More insight will be forthcoming.

Gebo in the twenty fourth stead indicates a gift bestowed on him from a spiritual source. This is probably in the form of insight which enables him more true freedom but will come with the obligation to use it to help others in their spiritual evolution.

The Three Aetts - A 24 Rune Method

This method is closer to what has been recorded as traditional. Layout your white cloth (a square yard or metre) and cast the 24 rune staves from your lot box or empty them from your bag, onto the cloth surface. You will either have marked the cloth as illustrated or you will visualise the divisions (see Fig. 9). The three concentric circles are the Nornic Matrix. The three wedges are the intersection of the cyclic evolutionary progressions as signified by the Aetts. For easy reference, these are:

Freyja's Eight: The awakening of 'The Self': The individual and collective social journey in the world - understanding Orlog - "That which has become".

Hagal's Eight: The testing of 'The Self': The individual and collective psychological journey - experiencing Wyrd- "That which is becoming".

Tyr's Eight: The actualising of the 'The Self': individual and collective spiritual journey - intuiting Skuld - "That which shall (is obliged to) come".

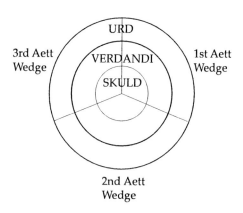

(Fig.9)

Some staves will be shown (exposed), others will be face down. Examine the distribution over the three spheres and the three wedges of influence. The visible staves, on top, are the ones to which you focus your primary attention. Secondary influences are read by the staves that are underneath or partly obscured by the top staves. When these runes are hidden, face down, read them after you have noted the primary runes. Turn them over from right to left, as you would turn the pages of a book, so to maintain their original position. This will reveal the Shinning Staves - upright and the Shadow Staves - inverted and reversed runes, as they were cast. They can be read as influences that are not obvious to the querist, or as influences not yet manifested.

Note also staves that are touching and those that overlap the spheres and wedges. Let your contemplative state form patterns of groupings and relate these to each other.

This method of reading is an advanced form and takes considerable focus - a development of both knowledge and intuition - to become proficient, but for runers who wish a holistic perception of Wyrd's Well/Web, its practice is worth the endeavour. The same principles apply to this method as to the simpler methods of reading. Rather than give an example reading of Cloth casting, I will leave it to the reader to experiment when they feel they are ready to attempt it.

The Wolf's Hook - A Nine Rune Method

This method was developed to gain a personal insight into the state of "the self" as described in the chapter on Soul Lore. The querist needs to be familiar with these concepts before attempting the casting. The Rede given is meant to provide a profound basis for meditation. The stead positions are meant to represent the Hvels or Wheels of the psycho-somatic complex as well as the individual aspects that holistically make up the particular entity.

The Wolf's Hook was a device of metal used to capture wolves much like a hook for fishing. Its shape is based on the Eihwaz rune stave - a symbol of both life and death. It is also similar to the shape of the Fylfot or Swastika which is associated with the god Thorr - symbolic of his mighty hammer Mjollnir in swirling motion which is then called the Sun Wheel.

As each reading will be totally unique, I will not attempt to give an example. The procedure is straight forward. Layout the runes as in the sequence shown (Fig.10) then contemplate the relationships on the vertical axis followed by the those on the horizontal axis.

228

(Fig.10)

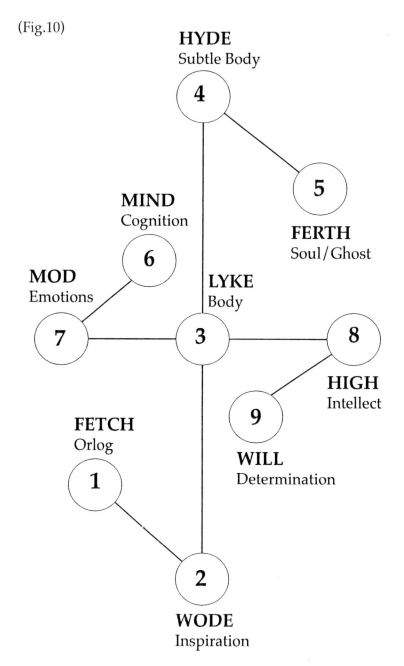

HYDE
Subtle Body

4

5

FERTH
Soul/Ghost

MIND
Cognition

6

MOD
Emotions

LYKE
Body

7

3

8

HIGH
Intellect

9

FETCH
Orlog

WILL
Determination

1

2

WODE
Inspiration

230

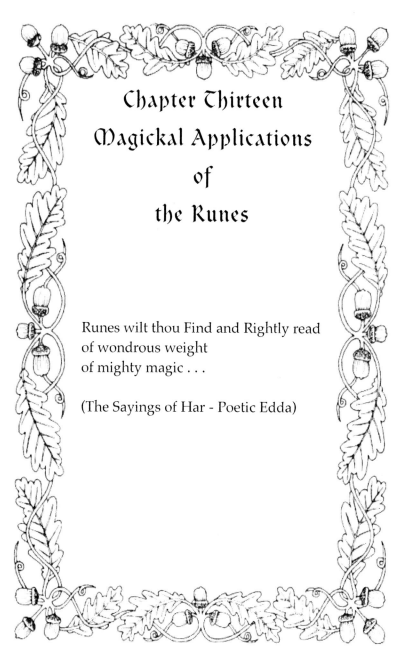

Chapter Thirteen
Magickal Applications
of
the Runes

Runes wilt thou Find and Rightly read
of wondrous weight
of mighty magic . . .

(The Sayings of Har - Poetic Edda)

232

Chapter Thirteen
Magickal Applications of the Runes

What is Magick?

Many definitions have been given of magick. Basically it is use of concentrated desire and determination - the Will - to affect changes in a chosen environment. The environment may be internally subjective - the consciousness/body of the magician - the "self" or externally subjective - the "self" of another. It may also be the objective environment of the individual - that which has a supportive or destructive affect for the person or the objective environment of the collective - that which has a supportive or destructive affect for friends, family, tribe, clan, nation.

Because of our sensual nature, we seemed to be most impressed with spectacular changes within the objective environment. Many years of fairy tales and now the 'special FX' of motion pictures have conditioned us to expect this expression of Magick - the sudden and seemingly supernatural alterations in reality. But even though this is possible by advanced Runemasters, it is not the measure of magick. In occult circles the changes to the external objective environment are considered **lesser** magick while affecting changes within the internal subjective (the self) and external subjective environment (other selves) are considered **greater** magick.

This may seem perplexing but when you consider that you are the centre of your particular universe within the greater multiverse, you come to the understanding that all changes in your life/environment originate within your own consciousness; through desires/actions whether you are aware or ignorant of your true motivations. It is at this point that I recommend you to re-read chapter four; Time and Probability. You have your particular Orlog which has been shaped by all that has gone before. So has your family, tribe, clan and nation of origin. So has the world of Midgard with all its inhabitants no matter what species.

When you change your awareness, you change your way of thinking, feeling and acting. When unconscious patterns of motivation and behaviour become conscious, you alter your comprehension of both the subjective and objective world. This peceptual alteration facilitates extended options for action. This is the divinatory - the Rede - function of the runes which is in itself truly magickal.

The runes are symbols of Orlog and Wyrd analogous to the language of computer software used to write an Operating System program. The practical use of runes for magick is taking these same symbols of insight and directing them towards affecting the desired changes.

With this computer program analogy the runes are a Meta-language with which we write in alterations to the directory which is called Orlog, specifically the configuration called Verdhandi (that which is becoming). If an alteration is made in the Operating System then the function and display of other Applications (interdependent programs), eg. intuition, reasoning and synchronous awareness, will be altered.

Simply said; by writing in changes to the Operating System of Orlog (that which is) you alter, extend or concentrate the capabilities of the Application called Skuld (that which is obliged to come) - your Wyrd.

Methods of Practice

Traditionally, there are two main branches of Magick in the Northern Way. One branch is called *Galdr* (ON) or Galdar (singing) and involves the directing of runic energy through archetypical identification with a god form eg. Odhinn - chanting, visualising and risting by the intention - the will power alone - of the magician. Its most common application is to increase personal power/knowledge/wisdom to facilitate the fulfilment of specific goals including warding energy to maintain freedom. Also the ability to influence others directly to work your will through the charisma of presence and speech. In Old Norse the male practitioner is called a *Vitki*, the female a *Vitka* and in Old English the cognates are *Wicca* and *Wicce* respectively. This magick is associated with the Æsir - god/esses of consciousness/intellect.

The other branch is called *Seidhr* (ON) or Seith (seething) also known as *Fiolkyngi* (great wisdom of the folk) and involves the spell chanting, rune risting, visualisation and the evocation of external entities god/esses and/or spirits eg. Freyja; Dwarfs; Elves, to achieve the desired result. The practice of *Spae* (ON) (scrying - clairvoyance); prediction of Orlog/Wyrd and out-of-body journeying (faring forth) is a part of Seith. This magick is of an elemental kind having to do with understanding and manipulating natural phenomena. Cursing and healing are integral to this practice. Most practitioners are women and in Old Norse are called *Voelva* (seeress) or *Vitt* (witch). Male practitioners are called *Seithmadr* (seething man).This magick is associated with the Vanir. Seith is akin to shamanism while Galdar is akin to Ritual Magick. Because Seith often involves trance states it is labelled as a passive/submissive thus a feminine form of magick (in the sense of being "Yin" as in Taoism) while Galdar is performed from an active/aggressive point of consciousness thus a masculine form (in the sense of being "Yang" as in Taoism). In the *Ylingasaga* it is written:

"Freyja was the daughter of Njorth. She was priestess at bless-ings, *blotgythia*. She first taught seith, which was usual to the Vanir, to the Esir."

and

"Odin knew this art, that brings great might, and worked it himself. It is called seith, and by its might he knew the Orlogs of men and understood silent lots. He could work the banes of men or loss of *hamingia* or waning health. So also could he take wit and power from some people and give them to others. But this *fiolkyngi*, as it is worked, involves such great *ergi* (passive receptiveness) that it is thought by manly men to be the most shameful way to go, and this art was learned by *gythia* (priest-esses)".

(trans. by James A. Chisholm)

The difference between the two forms are not cut and dried. They do overlap to a great extent. By the end of the Viking Age and during the conversion to Christianity, the differences are not apparent. Literary references lump all folk magick under the heading of *Fiolkyngi* - Seith. It is really a matter of applica-tion of intent rather than a distinction of practice. According to these categories, rune divination or scrying would be classified as Seith and so would Shape-Shifting (taking on the form or "borrowing" the subtle shape of an animal) yet these skills are also a part of Galdar practice. For our purposes it is most easiest to tentatively categorise Galdar as Shinning Usage and Seith as Shadow Usage. The reader should allow natural inclinations to be their guide in these matters.

To affect changes one must have "one pointedness" - an unwavering desire for the result to manifest but this is not enough in itself. The aspects of the self such as Mind, Will, Mood and High must be harmoniously directed towards the same goal. This is an appropriate time to re-read chapter three; Soul Lore. Regular meditation puts the runer in touch with the

Orthanc and will unlock ancestral memory which is very helpful for the application of rune wisdom in practice.

Rune magick has many aspects. Before attempting any practice the runer should consider these words of Odhinn from the *Havamal* (Poetic Edda):

"Know you how to carve them?

Know you how to read them?

Know you how to paint them?

Know you how to prove them?

Know you how to pray with them?

Know you how to blood-sacrifice with them?

Know you how to send with them?

Know you how to offer with them?

It is better not to pray

then to blood-sacrifice too much -

a gift always looks for recompense. It is better not to send than to offer too much - ..."

(trans. by Marijane Osborn & Stella Longland, Rune Games, Routledge-Keegan Paul 1982).

The runer most know that primal laws (Orlog) apply to the use of magick which is really a form of subtle physics. For every action that is Orlog their will be a reaction that is Skuld. Rune Lore says that you have to pledge action or service in exchange for what you desire to become a reality. You have to have a reason or goal for the use of the energy you wish to manifest.

This is particularly true of Seith Magick where there is interaction with external entities whose help is called upon. In exchange for this gift, one must render a price. This price agreed upon in your intent will be exacted whether you change your mind or not. The warning here is to be sure you are willing to pay the fee - remember the tale of the Pied Piper of Hamlein.

The metaphorical image of the Web is appropriate here also. Every thread of focused will woven into the subtle fabric of the collective unconscious binds itself to, and alters, the pattern of the whole. Alternatively, when runes are willfully visualised /risted/sung their subtle energy drops into the Well of Wyrd to form a layer in the Orlog which will shape the present and that 'which is becoming'. None of us know exactly what other changes we may wrought in the Wyrd by our workings or when they might manifest. The saw, "be careful what you wish for because you may just get it", applies in this case for this saw describes the acts of syncronicity that happen in our lives when we least expect them, sometimes years after we have forgotten our desires. Sometimes by then, their fulfilment may be unwanted and the manifestation can cause problems. Because of our "instant gratification" society we expect our magick to manifest when we want it - usually immediately. This is not how things work. Time and Probability must be taken into account.

It is important to be specific in your request and to set time limitations on the manifestation of your will. Of all the probabilities in the Well, we are focusing on what we want to be, how and when. With the Web of Wyrd analogy, we are weaving the threads to intersect the probability factors in our favour. Then we forget about it and get on with our lives. By continually mulling over a desire but not sending it into the Well - not releasing it, we are holding the desire in stasis. This will cause fatigue and accomplish little. It is like an archer with a drawn bow - the arrow is aimed at the target but s/he wont let go. What happens then? S/he starts to hurt with the strain and their attention and aim wavers with the fatigue.

Emotion is a powerful source of magickal energy. It engages the Mod and invokes the Wode. Emotion can be all consuming and while we are in its grip we have "one pointedness". It is good to excite the emotions and utilise the senses in ecstatic conditions eg. trance, for magick but just before we reach mental (or physical) orgasm we must harness this volcanic energy and direct it through our Will - the sending; point of release (the archer releases the arrow and then relaxes their posture).

Areas of Application

In the *Havamal*, Odhinn says he knows eighteen lays of power. These are rune/seith spells:

I know those lays
Which no ruler's wife knows,
Nor any man's son.
Help one is called,
And it will help you
Against sorrows and trials
And every grief there is.

I know the second,
Which those sons of men need
Who wish to live as healers.

I know the third:
If my need grows dire
for fetters on my deadly foes,
I dull the blades
Of my enemies -
Neither weapons nor wiles will bite for them.

I know this, the fourth:
If warriors lock up
My shoulder-limbs,
I chant thus,
And I can go;
The fetters spring from my feet,
And the shackles from my hands.

I know this, the fifth:
If I see an arrow flit in battle,
Shot deadly straight,
None flies so hard
I cannot halt it
If I catch sight of it.

I know this, the sixth:
If a thane conjures me
On the roots of a raw sapling,
The man
Who calls down curses on me -
Misfortunes will consume him, rather than me.

I know this, the seventh:
If I see a high hall Blazing around benchmates,
None burns so broad
That I cannot save them:
I know the spell to chant.

I know this, the eighth:
Which is useful
For everyone to learn
Whose hate waxes

240

For a war-king's sons:
I can soon remedy that.

I know this, the ninth:
If I stand in need
Of keeping my ship afloat,
I can calm the wind
Smooth the waves,
And lull all the sea to sleep.

I know this, the tenth:
If I see hedge-riders
Witching aloft,
I so work it
That they go astray
of their own skins,
Of their own souls.

I know this, the eleventh:
If I must lead
Old friends to battle,
I chant under their shields,
And they go with power,
Safe to war,
Safe from war,
Safe wherever they are.

I know this, the twelfth:
If I see aloft in a tree
A noosed-up corpse swinging,
Thus I carve
And I paint in runes

So that the man steps down
And speaks with me.

I know this, the thirteenth:
If I should cast water on
A young thane,
He will not fall;
No matter if he goes to war
The hero will not sink under swords.

I know this, the Fourteenth:
If I should preach the gods
Before assembled troops,
I will know how to distinguish
All Aesir and elves:
Few of the unwise know this.

I know this, the fifteenth,
Which the dwarf Thjothrerir
Chanted before Delling's (the dwarf glowing = dawn) doors.
He chanted power to Aesir,
And prowess to elves,
And foresight to Hropta-Tyr (Odinn).

I know this, the sixteenth:
If I wish to have all the clever woman's
High spirits and games,
I steal the heart
Of a white-armed wench
And I turn all her thoughts.

I know this, the seventeenth:

242

So that the young girl
Will be loath to shun me.
Loddfafnir (cunning trickster?), you will
Be long in learning
These lays,
Though they will do you good if you get them,
Be useable if you grasp them,
Handy if you have them.

I know this, the eighteenth,
Which never will I teach Maid or man's wife
(All is better
Which one understands alone -
The end of the lays follows),
Except that woman
Who folds me in her arms,
Or maybe my sister.

(trans. by Marijane Osborn & Stella Longland, et al).

The 1st is to alleviate grief of any kind. The 2nd is to empower Healers. The 3rd is to fetter (bind or stop) enemies plans and weapons as to be of no harm. The 4th is to release fetters, physical and other, placed on one by an enemy - to free one's self. The 5th stops projectiles from reaching their intended mark. The 6th returns runic curses upon their sender. The 7th saves those trapped by fire. The 8th removes hate from men's hearts. The 9th calms the wind and seas and prevents boats from sinking. The 10th kills shape-shifters and witches who are operating in their Hydes (subtle bodies) by severing the Athem (connecting cord of soul and body). The 11th wards physical protection in battle. The 12th is for necromancy. It forces the spirit of a hanged dead body to speak to the runer. The 13th is for warding and uses the casting of water on another to stop them from sinking - either metaphorically or in reality. The 14th gives the ability to know all about the Æsir Gods and Elves. The 15th is the source of power for the Gods, prowess for the Elves and the precognitive ability of Odhinn. The 16th enables a man to control a woman through her falling in love with him. The 17th invokes lust in young girls for the spell wielder. The 18th is a secret (whispered in the dead god Baldar's ear on his funeral pyre) - maybe to recall previous rebirths through the agency of the Fetch and/or personal Valkyrie?

Magickal Lore

The magickal meanings given are presented as positive in that they are used to aid the individual and the collective. However, the use of runes can just as easily be used for negative purposes.

In his book *The Elements of the Runes*, Bernard King investigates the inversion or perversion of runic energy with what is called Troll Runes (Trolls being a type of Giant). This is the use of the Thurisaz rune in this manner is to invoke the polarity function of any singular stave or group of rune staves by risting the Thurisaz rune before the others, eg. ᚦ : ᚠ. In this case instead of attracting or sending wealth, it would attract poverty, block the acquisition of wealth or incite greed. So to perceive the polarity application of the rune stave, all is needed is to comprehend the given meanings. Whether the normal (unobstructed) or perverted (obstructed) meanings of the runes can be called good or evil is a matter of intent and application. Magickal energy is neutral and any ethical or moral judgement on, or consequence of, their use is up to the individual runer.

The warning has already been given by Odhinn himself. In keeping with the terminology we have used in this book to describe runes, we will call their unobstructed use Shinning and their obstructed use Shadow. The reader is encouraged to

244

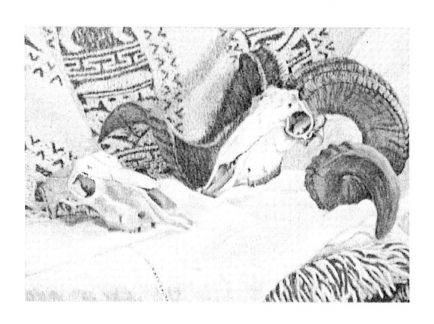

review the Key Words in the Aetts, chapters 7,8,9 to stimulate additional possible magickal applications.

Freyja's Aett:

ᚠ (Fehu):
Magickal meaning: "Initiating Personal Power in Self and in the World".

Shinning usage: Attracting aid, attracting wealth, invoking philanthropy, erotic stimulation, channelling Solar energy, increasing psychic powers, projecting/sending spells.

Shadow usage: Blocking help, attracting poverty, creating greed, damning libido, causing lassitude, undermining psychic abilities, blocking spells.

ᚢ (Uruz):
Magickal meaning: "Expanding and Protecting Self-Interest ".

Shinning usage: Curing disease - realigning causal energies to their natural flow, increasing health and fitness both psychological and physical, building self-esteem and assertiveness, increasing luck (speed), aligning self with telluric currents (the energy of Ley lines).

Shadow usage: Causing disease, disrupting metabolic processes, evoking insecurity and aggression, disturbing natural earth currents.

ᚦ (Thurisaz):
Magickal meaning: "Resisting Degeneration and Dissolution".

Shinning usage: Strengthening the will, defending integrity, regenerating form, overcoming inhibitions and psychological chaos, enhancing sexual attraction in males, warding against elemental spirits.

246

Shadow usage: Weakening the will, dissolving integrity, degenerating form, inciting fear/defencelessness, inducing psychological distress/chaos, inciting lust, invoking spirits to attack.

ᚨ (Ansuz):
Magickal meaning: "Agitation of Mind and Mood".

Shinning usage: Transmission of feeling/emotions into thought/words, enhancement of Galdar ability, gaining direct inspiration, intellectual clarity, power of persuasion, overcoming impediments to success, breaking the fetters of anxiety and/or phobias, accessing numinous knowledge, control of elemental air.

Shadow usage: Inhibiting expression of feelings/emotions/thoughts, confusion of mental states, dulling of intellect, evoking gullibility, hypnotic suggestion creating impediments to action, fettering enemies with anxiety, phobias or curses, inciting wind storms.

ᚱ (Raidho):
Magickal meaning: "Extending Control through Right Action".

Shinning usage: Transmission of plans/desires into action, evoking ethical responsibility, gaining correct advice, enhancing foresight, deflecting attacks, assuring right judgement in legal matters, increasing power through ritual activity, understanding natural cycles, maintaining freedom of movement.

Shadow usage: Blocking motivation, creating internal inertia, stimulating irrational thought and behaviour, ignoring advice, distorting perception, increasing vulnerability, inducing frustration through routine, stimulating destructive storm activity, enforcing relocation.

< **(Kenaz):**
Magickal meaning: "Recognition of Connective Relationships".

Shinning usage: Perceiving motivations and actions of others, penetrating illusionary projections, returning runic curses to their source, evoking hidden knowledge/skills/creativity, counteracting toxicity in the environment and body, eg. blood cleansing, evoking healthy sexual desire - the will to reproduce.

Shadow usage: Hiding motivations and actions, creating illusionary projections, sending runic curses, evoking creative blockages - ignorance, inducing environmental and personal toxicity, eg. boils, distorting sexual desire - deviance.

X **(Gebo):**
Magickal meaning: "Binding of Individuals into Mutual Dependence".

Shinning usage: Counteracting ill will, attracting generosity, contracting unions, increasing harmony within families, acquiring wisdom of expectation and reward, increasing influence in material and spiritual realms, enhancing sex magick, personal warding from the elemental of fire.

Shadow usage: Inciting ill will, generating meanness, disrupting contractual arrangements, evoking disharmony, stimulating non-discrimination of cause and effect, causing loss of favour, sexually dominating - vampirism, causing "spontaneous combustion" or inciting arson.

P **(Wunjo):**
Magickal meaning: "Using the Collective to gain Individual Fulfilment".

Shinning usage: Healing estrangement, stimulating aware-ness of hidden enemies/danger, gaining acceptance of peers, achieving social/spiritual peace, gaining wish fulfilment, binding supportive energies for specific purpose, eg. the runes.

Shadow usage: Inciting animosity, causing ignorance of hidden enemies/danger, creating alienation, stimulating rage/frenzy, frustrating fulfilment of desires, disrupting cohesion of magickal focus - weakening spells.

Hagal's Aett:

ᚺ (Hagalaz):
Magickal meaning: "Utilising Disruption for Self-Evaluation".

Shinning usage: Counteracting hatred, protection from unexpected attack, evoking comfort during crisis, eliciting smooth transitions between events, stimulating mystical experience, developing insight into evolutionary process, exorcising demonic possession, warding from hail, flood and winter storms - control of elemental water / wind combination.

Shadow usage: Inciting hatred, invoking sudden attack, evoking misery and depression, causing maladjustment, arousing psychosis, inciting demonic possession, causing hail, floods and winter storms - agitation of elemental water / wind combination..

ᚾ (Nauthiz):
Magickal meaning: "Acknowledging and Removing Limitations".

Shinning usage: Uncovering "weregild" - unacknowledged obligations, debts to others, exposing problem areas in own life, overcoming fear, stimulating incisive action, psycho-somatic healing, slaying of psychic attackers, protecting against drought, plague and forest fires.

Shadow usage: Restricting others through hidden obliga-tions, amplifying existing problems, fettering through fear, causing inaction, stimulating psycho-somatic illness, initiating psychic attack, invoking drought, plague and wildfire.

| (Isa): Magickal meaning:
"Isolating the Self to Preserve Integrity".

Shinning usage: Stabilising of individual consciousness - self containment, consolidating ego integrity, eliciting respect and support, halting unwanted stimulation and/or attention, shielding in all environments, amplifying concentration and will power, breaking inertia, controlling spirits.

Shadow usage: Destabilising internal integrity, invoking self-absorption and loneliness, disintegrating ego boundaries, causing self loathing, attracting unwanted attention and treachery, placing in danger through loss of perception, fettering by delusion, sending hauntings.

❖ (Jera):
Magickal meaning: "Timing as a Framework for Manifestation".

Shinning usage: Enhancing visualisation and projection, invoking synchronisation of time and events, stabilising bio-rhythms, eg. menstrual period, accelerating manifestation of goals, invoking a bumper harvest or plenty, completing life lessons, bridging the worlds of life and death.

Shadow usage: Dimming the ability to 'tune in', evoking bad timing, disrupting bio-rhythms, eg. uncontrollable period bleeding, inducing repetition without progression, causing famine or shortage, inducing the transference of spirit into dead matter - necromantic reawakening.

∫ (Eihwaz):
Magickal meaning: "Initiating a free flow of consciousness within the Psyche".

Shinning usage: Inducing spiritual initiation, gaining

250

spiritual protection, unlocking the individual and collective unconscious (personal and ancestral memories etc.), connecting with the superconscious, evoking psychic flexibility and emotional endurance, gaining experience of "the self", exploring alternate realities (Nine Worlds).

Shadow usage: Causing retreat from life trials, amplifying spiritual vulnerability, evoking painful repressed memories, invoking fear of death, amplifying neurotic tendencies, encouraging superficial awareness, fettering of evolutionary drive.

⚸ (Perthro):
Magickal meaning: "Accessing Hamingja - the hidden store of power and luck".

Shinning usage: Accessing secret knowledge (Well of Wyrd), divining and scrying to read Orlog, unravelling neurotic bindings, inducing easy childbirth, drawing on accumulated might (personal and ancestral), releasing hidden potential into manifestation - increasing fortuitous opportunities, fixing magickal will into Well and Web - rune risting.

Shadow usage: Hiding secret activities, evoking false sense of well being, inducing over indulgence/addictions, causing birthing problems, eg. stillborn, dissipation of personal luck, cursing family lines, invoking destruction of sexual intimacy and familial relationships.

ᛉ (Elhaz):
Magickal meaning: "Appropriate Action through Evolutionary Impetus".

Shinning usage: Connecting with higher beings, shielding during 'Faring Forth', enhancing precognitive ability, channelling power of the three highest realms (Asgard, Vanaheim, Asgard) into self - increasing hamingja, accelerating self healing, creating sanctuary, enlisting benefactors.

Shadow usage: Disconnecting divine link, invoking defencelessness, dulling foresight, invoking the energy of the three lower realms (Hel, Niflheim, Muspellheim); draining hamingja, causing death, removing support, inciting betrayal.

∫ (Sowilo):
Magickal meaning: "Removing Illusions and Obstructions to Advancement".

Shinning usage: Illuminating direct pathways to enlightenment, enhancing skill of discrimination leading to success, accessing inner guidance, amplifying will power, removing obstructions to realisation of goals, stimulating psychosomatic centres - wheels, (*hvels*,ON and *chakra*,Sanskrit) stimulating libido/attraction, gaining swift victory.

Shadow usage: Distracting from chosen path, increasing gullibility, choosing wrong advice, weakening will, pursuing goals set by others, inhibiting flow of energy through the psychosomatic centres, losing purpose, inciting sexual infatuation, inciting electrical storms/lightning.

Tyr's Aett:

↑ (Tiwaz):
Magickal meaning: "Asserting Authority to Gain and Maintain Control".

Shinning usage: Building stamina/character/authority, arousing collective and personal compromise,inducing order and calm, gaining justice through Orlog (letter of the law), strengthening faith in magickal/religious instinct, enhancing martial skills/strength, gaining success in enterprise and victory in conflict, evoking trust and admiration.

Shadow usage: Weakening will, undermining trust/authority, evoking unnecessary sacrifice, arousing disorder/strife, creating injustice, undermining faith in magickal/religious instinct, fettering skills of enemies, invoking failure in enterprise and defeat in conflict, inciting lust/hero worship.

ᛒ (Berkano):
Magickal meaning: "Containing and Utilising the Collective Integrity ".

Shinning usage: Binding associated objects/ideas, containing secrecy, unleashing stored ancestral memory/wisdom, ensuring domestic tranquillity, protecting the unborn/children, healing grief/depression, curing female illnesses, increasing fertility, rejuvenating the life force, bringing to fruition creative impetus, accessing life/death mysteries; journeying to the underworld of Hel/Niflheim.

Shadow usage: Scattering knowledge of linkages, exposing secrets, locking access to the folk-collective unconscious, inciting domestic friction, exposing the unborn/children to danger, amplifying grief/depression, aggravating female illnesses, invoking sterility, withering the life force, inciting abandonment of projects, invoking ignorance/fear of life/death mysteries; forgetfulness of other rebirths.

ᛖ (Ehwaz):
Magickal meaning: "Maintaining Co-ordination during Psychological Transitions".

Shinning usage: Invoking a sense of certainty to the will, harmonising internal masculine/feminine energies, harmonising emotional/sexual relationships, controlling psychosomatic reactions, enhancing close external co-operative functioning, gaining internal spiritual guidance, enabling swift journeys, shifting-shape of Hyde, faring forth between the worlds.

Shadow usage: Invoking a sense of uncertainty/doubt, Disrupting harmony of internal masculine/feminine energies, rupturing emotional/sexual relationships, disturbing psychosomatic integrity, causing strife among teamworkers, blocking internal guidance, fettering journeys, attacking the hyde/athem connection in others, causing disorientation during out-of-body experiences.

ᛗ (Mannaz):
Magickal meaning: "Superseding the Limitations of Nature".

Shinning usage: Differentiating between Instinct and Mind, balancing human polar nature, opening the "mind's eye", increasing general mental powers and practical abilities, overcoming adversity, enhancing legal proceedings, induce co-operation for collective benefit, invoke close friendships, sussing out and undermining enemies, invoke powers of the natural world into the magician.

Shadow usage: Invoking instinct over reason, enhancing unbalanced perception, closing off spiritual insight, causing general dullness and ineptitude, causing adversity, turn legal proceedings against one, evoking selfishness and non-cooperation, hiding false friendships, inciting revenge, inciting baseness.

ᛚ (Laguz):
Magickal meaning: "Conducting the Life-Force to Manifest Your Will".

Shinning usage: Increasing vitality and charisma, influencing others to obtain help, collecting unformed magickal energy for shaping, increasing positive emotions, eg. love, enhancing perception of primal law (orlog) - developing "second sight", control of elemental water.

Shadow usage: Withering of life force and personal magnetism, invading mind and dream states, draining stored etheric energy from another - vampirism, evoking depression and emotional chaos, blocking "second sight", causing floods and/or drought.

◇ **(Ingwaz):**
Magickal meaning: "Concentration of Accumulated Power for Future Manifestation".

Shinning usage: Storing power for future use, releasing reserved power for transformation, transferring personal or family hamingja (accumulated magickal luck), binding magickal energies together over time, faring forth to world of Vanaheim , evoking male fertility, creating a magick mirror, casting a working sanctuary - *Vè* (ON) or *Wihstead* (OE).

Shadow usage: Fettering the use of accumulated power or hamingja, binding others spells, invoking nature spirits into Midgard, stimulating male lust, spying on others clairvoyantly, blocking access to spiritual sanctuary.

◊ **(Othala):**
Magickal meaning: "Accessing Power from the Individual and Collective Folk-Conscious".

Shinning usage: Accessing hereditary wisdom/hamingja, enhancing nobility and cultural pride, maintaining clanic custom, order and security, protecting personal freedom and property, attracting and preserving material inheritance, preserving alliances, attracting personal allegiance and bene-factors, enhancing personal authority, attracting wealth through property, invoking a ritual runic sanctuary - *Vè* or *Wihstead*, clairvoyantly viewing the 'past'.

Shadow usage: Severing of psychic/ethnic continuity, stimulating prejudice and racial intolerance, eliciting break-down of clanic customs/values and security, evoking loss of freedom and poverty, causing loss of material inheritance, breaking of alliances, causing loss of favour, stimulating abuse of authority, invoking bad real estate investments, causing vagrancy.

ᛞ (Dagaz):
Magickal meaning: "Transcendence of Individual and Collective Definition".

Shinning usage: Reconcilliating the polar paradox of spirit / matter - invoking integration of consciousness, experiencing the mystical "moment" - enlightenment, gaining transpersonal inspiration, understanding of synchronicity, stimulating rapid polarity change - creating new   beginnings, righting of wrongs, opening the "third eye",   accessing the elemental power of light, creating an invisibility shield.

Shadow usage: Invoking non-resolution of mental conflict, creating ignorance and ennui, engineering ironic situations, causing sudden reversals of fortune, missing opportunities, blocking mystical awareness, stimulating cataclysmic change, invoking fire for destructive purposes.

Preparation for Magickal Work

No matter what form your magick is going to take, it is important that you prepare yourself and the chosen space for your activity by separation from everyday concerns. The reason for this is simply to prevent distractions and interruptions to your concentration.

Any objects you will use in the magick should be placed in the working area before hand - such as paper, pens, paint, brushes, wood, risting tools, knife, cauldrons, incense, candles.

The runes you will be using and the method of the working should be clear in your mind. Traditionally, the runes selected for empowerment were used in the chants as well as the charm. This means for example, that you might use a repetition of the Wunjo stave (ᚹ) = W, the Wish fulfilment rune in the primary invocation of your Will. You may be desiring to remove self-ignorance and strengthen your will in the face of adversity, so you had chosen the Sowilo rune ($\lessgtr$) = S to incorporate into your statement of purpose. You may decide to combine these runes with others into your charm to form a Bind-Rune - a symbol of your willed intent (see below).

Most runers spend time before hand working out exactly the flow of the ritual events by visualisation. This has the purpose of allowing the actual working to unravel itself without constant distraction from the analytical practices of the mind. It enhances the concentration of the will/emotions on the purpose. It is important to remember that by engaging all the senses, mind and emotion in your actual working you are focusing your "one-pointedness" and increasing the potency and probability of magickal success.

Take a shower and change your clothes. If you have a special garment that helps you to separate your attention from work-a-day concerns then put it on. Seat yourself in the area and do deep breathing and allow yourself to slip into a meditative state. This is quickly achieved by concentration on or by chanting of the Isa (|) rune for 15 to 20 minutes (for a more detailed meditation technique see the Eihwaz Contemplation at the end of this chapter). Then fix your mind on the purpose and desired result of your working. You may also evoke emotions that help you to focus on your particular need.

Working

With both Galdar and Seith, an area is symbolically claimed as an extension of "the self". This area is called a *Vè* (ON) or *Wihstead* (OE) - "sacred enclosure" ($\diamondsuit$). It can be a circle, a triangle or a diamond shape. It can be marked out physically or just visualised. Then the enclosure is warded by using a protective sigil.

In this case the rune stave (ᛉ) is signed while evoking the thought of separating and protecting the area from all unwanted intrusion. This is done to the four quarters, going clockwise, in the order of North, South, East and West for Galdar magick. For Seith magick; East, South, West and North. For Shadow Usage, the signing may be done in a counter clockwise direction. In German, this practice is known as *Widerschinden* ([going] contrary [for the purpose of making something] decrease, decline or disappear).

It is now appropriate for you to invoke your will. If you choose the Galdar way, you may wish to evoke the archetypical energy of identification with a power source of special significance to you, eg. Odhinn as Runemaster. You may chant your memorised lay (or be spontaneous in your calling), such as:

Woden Within

Woden Without,

From The Windy Tree,

I Shout!

The Nine Worlds Know

My Need,

Into Both Well and Web,

With Victory,

I Rist My Deed!

With the will now activated the runer goes on to the next stage of stating/chanting the purpose of the working. In this example, for a continuing development of self-awareness and strong character through the lessons of this incarnation - the trials and tribulations of life:

258

From This Turning,

Till The End Of My Life,

Knowledge Of Self,

And Strength Through Strife!

Before going to the next stage let's examine the chants in more detail especially to see the runic substitution with the 'bolded' first letters of each word. It may first appear difficult to comprehend the complexity but remember that if you have planned your ritual words of power, you would have constructed them to enhance the runic thrust of your will.

ᚹ oden ᚹ ithin

ᚹ oden ᚹ ithout,

ᚠ rom ᛏ he ᚹ indy ᛏ ree,

ᛁ ᛋ hout!

ᛏ he ᚾ ine ᚹ orlds ᚲ now,

ᛗ y ᚾ eed,

ᛁ nto ᛒ oth ᚹ ell ᚠ nd ᚹ eb,

ᚹ ith ᚺ ictory,

ᛁ ᚱ ist ᛗ y ᛗ eed!

ᚠ rom ᛏ his ᛏ urning,

ᛏ ill ᛏ he ᛍ nd ᛟ f ᛗ y ᛚ ife,

ᚲ nowledge ᛟ f ᛋ elf,

ᚠ nd ᛋ trength ᛏ hrough ᛋ trife!

If you take these runes and write them in the line order and triple grouping that you have written the chants, you will now have a risted runic charm of your intent (as an exercise review each rune's magickal meaning and note the emphasis on certain staves through repetition):

: ᚹ ᚹ ᚹ ᚹ : ᚠ ᛏ ᚹ ᛏ : ᛁ ᛋ :
: ᛏ ᛄ ᚹ ᚲ : ᛗ ᛄ : ᛁ ᛒ ᚹ ᚠ ᚹ : ᚦ ᚢ : ᛁ ᚱ ᛗ ᛗ :
: ᚠ ᛏ ᛏ : ᛏ ᛏ ᛗ ᛩ ᛗᛚ : ᚲ ᛩ ᛋ : ᚠ ᛋ ᛏ ᛋ :

This can be the some total of your working if you choose or you may decide to focus the essential elements of your intent. In that case you may decide to select ᚹ - the wish fulfilment rune; ᛋ - the rune of guidance/removal of ignorance; ᚻ - the rune of strength and ᛏ - the rune of victory. You now have four rune staves. A cross reference with the number lore in the chapter on The Runic Code gives this information on the number 4 : "Suspension, the controlled balance of opposing and harmonious forces. The mastery of material energy". The fourth rune is Ansuz - ᚠ and its magickal meaning is "Agitation of Mind and Mood". If you add up the numerical order value of the four runes:

ᚹ = 8;   ᛋ = 16;   ᚻ = 2;   ᛏ = 17 you get 43 which can be broken down to 4 (ᚠ) + 3 (ᚦ) = 7 (ᚷ); In Number Lore - **"Conscious supernatural awareness, existential mysteries".**

Are these the energies you are intent on manifesting? If the answer is yes, then these runes will serve your purpose.

You may now wish to shape a Bind-Rune (Fig.1) from these staves as a concentration of the working.

260

Magick is like distilling - the more concentrated you can get it the more powerful is the effect. Also, the more the runes are hidden from decoding by the analytical consciousness (left brain), the more powerful is the magick wrought through the intuitional consciousness (right brain). In other words, continual deciphering is like the archer who repetitively takes aim and calculating the target but doesn't release the arrow. With the construction of Bind-Runes, the consideration of inverted, reversed etc. does not apply as in divination. The aim is to concentrate the staves for the least number of apparent risting strokes but when you rist each rune, make sure that you do trace each stave completely even though it will not show in the final shape.

Order of Bind-Rune Construction

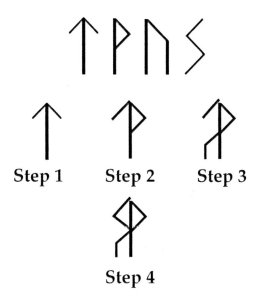

Fig. 1

The final concentration of your will is in this Bind-Rune (the possibilities for other combinations for Bind-Runes in magickal work can be explored only through experiment although other Rune Books such as Nigel Pennicks' *Rune Magic; The History and Practice of Ancient Runic Traditions* do give examples. Edred Thorsson's *Futhark; A handbook of Rune Magick* and *Discover Runes; Understanding and Using the Power of Runes* by Tony Willis are highly recommended).

You are now ready to do the "sending". This is the time for our patient archer to release the arrow towards its target. In this case your target is the Well of Wyrd. You may choose to view the elements as a doorway or a mental release alone. The simplest ways are often the best according to your level of magickal development. If you have risted the charm or bind-rune on paper or wood (in the same manner as described in the chapter ten; Crafting Your Own Runes), you can release it, ie. the sending, by casting it into a fire kindled for this purpose only. Either on the ground or in a cauldron. As it is burning concentrate on the purpose of your working with the knowledge that it is now completed and what you have focused on is now a reality. Released into the Well/Web by fire and air. This is important - in your consciousness you must hold that your will has already been realised. It is not something to come in some future - it is now a part of "what is". It is in the Well and Web and from this turning point you do not have to be concerned with its manifestation. It will make itself apparent.

The same applies if you choose to bury it, cast it on the water or just visualise the rune(s) being shot like and arrow. Now you can break your concentration by such acts as clapping the hands three times and/or by saying the like of:

"Thus the work is ended!"

Afterthought

You may choose to sit quietly for a while but remember, don't think about what you have just done. Engage your attention on externals - go for a walk or pick up a magazine or book, listen to music.

If your particular working involves a set period of time and you have decided to keep the charm/bind-rune on your person or in storage, don't forget to dispose of it through the elements at the set time of expiration. It is not good to have magickal power sources lying around still radiating their energy after the set time of the spells completion. They will interfere with your life whether you have forgotten or not.

Literary Examples of Seith

There are many recordings of seith practice in the Sagas. I have included some to give the reader a glimpse of the scope of the application of this magick:

"They put the intelligence of three men into the dog by means of seith. He barked twice but spoke every third word."

Saga of Hakon the Good (trans. by James A. Chisholm)

"That same night Eyvind Kelda came to the island with a fully manned longship. They were all seithmenn and men skilled in fiolkyngi. Eyvindr went away from the ship and the crew to work his fiolkyngi. He worked up for them such great darkness and fog, that the king and his host were unable to see them ...."

Saga of Olaf Tryggvason (trans. by James A. Chisholm)

"Thord came to Kotkell's dwelling with nine men. Kotkell's sons were not home. He then summonsed Kotkell, Grima and their sons for their thievery and fiolkyngi on the penalty of outlawry. He summoned them to the althing and then went to his ship. Then Hallbiorn and Stigandi came home as Thord was leaving the land and only a little ways. Kotkell told his sons what he had done. The brothers grew wroth over this and said that no man had ever contended with them with such hostility. Then Kotkell had great seith platform raised and they all climbed up into it. Then they chanted hard twisted lore that was galdar. Soon there was a great storm. Thord Ingunnarson and his men found this when they were out to sea, that a storm was sent against them...Afterwards a breaker rose close to the land where no one man had known one to have risen before, and it struck the ship and heaved the keel over. Thord and all his companions drowned there....They thought that death was fitting for working such fiolkyngi as Kotkell and his family had done...."

Laxdaela Saga (trans. by James A. Chisholm)

"Those with Ingiand worked seith according to ancient custom such that men sought their forlog from this. There a Finnish fiolkunning woman had come. Ingimund and Grim came to the feast with a great crowd. A splendid high seat was built for the finnish woman. Thence went men to ask, each of his concerns, and they asked about their orlog. She spaed (spied) for each as he came, but there were some who were not pleased. The sworn brothers sat in their room and did not go to enquire. They reclined and thought little of her spae. Volfan said: "Why do the young men not ask about their forlog, since to me it seems they are the noteworthy men among those who are gathered here?" Ingimund answered: "I do not wish to know my orlog faster than it unfolds and I do not think that my luck falls under your tongue roots." She answered: "Then I will tell you unasked that you will settle in a land called Iceland where wood does not grow. There you will become a man of rank and grow old. Your family will be large and renowned in that land...and that shall happen as I said, for there is a mark of this (the truth of her prophesy) in that the lot (idol) that king Harald gave you at Halfr-Frith is gone from your purse and has come to the same holt where you shall settle, the lot is a Frey marked of silver, and when you raise a homestead there the veracity of my words will be proved."

Vaetnsdale Saga (trans. by James A. Chisholm)

"Thurith Soundfiller and her son Volusteinn fared from Halogaland to Iceland and took Bolungavik and dwelled in Vatsness. She was called Soundfiller because whe worked seith such that during a famine in Halogaland that the sound was filled with fish."

Landnamabok (trans. by James A. Chisholm)

"Skuld was the greatest of Galdra-kind and of elvin stock on her mother's side.

At this time Skuld gathered to herself all the greatest men and also all the rabble of the nearby districts. This betrayal was kept secret so that King Hrolfr was not aware of any of it, nor did his retinue have any inkling about it because the greatest galdar was used. Skuld set herself to the greatest seith to overcome Hrolf her brother so that in her host were elves, norns, an untold number of other evil things, such that human power could not stand up to it.

The bear had now disappeared from the army and the battle started to encumber them. The Drighten Skuld did not work any tricks while the bear was in King Hrolf's host, there as she sat in her black tent upon her seith-hiallr. But things changed now as dim night follows bright day. King Hrolf's men now saw a huge boar coming out of King Hiorvarth's host: it was no smaller than an ox of three winters and was wolf-grey in color. (Note: Arrows fly from the boar's bristles.)

'Skuld's army is numerous,' said Bothvar, 'and I am afraid that the dead stir here and rise up again to fight against us, and it will be tough to fight with fetches'."

Hrolf Kraki Saga (trans. by James A. Chisholm)

"Hallgrim had a halberd on which he had lain seith so that no weapon would be able to kill him. Its magic power is such that one can know when a man is going to be killed by the great ringing noise it make."

Njàl's Saga (trans. by James A. Chisholm)

"She embraced him and Kissed him saying: "If I have the power over you it seems I do, then this (spell) which I lay on you will never have the pleasure of that woman whom you intend to have in Iceland."

Njàl's Saga (trans. by James A. Chisholm)

Fig.2

The Valknut

This is also called Valgrind (gate of the chosen - Fig.2). It is an archetypal symbol sacred to the cult of Odhinn and used for meditation, equivalent in function to the eastern mandalas in its potency to focus the consciousness on the mystical comprehension of the multiverse. Its three interlocking triangles embody the three realms or tiers and its nine sides the Nine Worlds. It is a unity of being expressing the eternal arising, unfolding and passing away of phenomena, only to begin again the cycle.

266

Eihwaz Contemplation: Techniques for Empowerment

The Wheels on the World Tree

A wealth of information is available on a variety of Meditation/Contemplation techniques but the Runer needs to focus his/her methods in way that supports their understanding of Runic Magick.

The primary mode of runic centring is the use of the Isa (|) rune for condensation of the ego to its innate condition of pure awareness. This awareness does not seek an object as its focus but allows itself to exist solely as "I am". It is understood by all practitioners of this way that this state allows the Wode principle to saturate the threshold of the subconscious mind and through the natural 'osmotic' effect gradually fill the daily consciousness with chthonic (Odinnic/Vaniric) knowledge. This inspiration gradually allows the runer to think/act on an almost instinctual level of appropriate reaction to the changes in the pattern of Wyrd in their lives.

When this meditation is practiced daily, especially in conjunction with Rune contemplation, the aspiring Vitki/Vitka begins to know when and how to approach both Galdar and Seith magick for the purpose of effecting changes in both or either the subjective and objective Multiverse.

Among the contemplation techniques for conscious empowerment, are those that require the Vitki (magician) to visualise the "doorways" through which these energies permeate the "multi-layered" entity that we identify as the "self". In most occult and mystical traditions these doorways are perceived as wheels (*Hvels*, ON and *Chakra*, Sanskrit) of spiralling energy, that are situated along a vertical axis, that corresponds to the spinal column in the body. These wheels act both as receivers/senders of energy from/to the Multiverse.

267

In runelore, the Eihwaz stave - ᛇ , is seen as the World Tree, Yggdrasil (Steed of the Terrible ie. Odhinn), Irminsul, (the Pillar of Heaven), which supports the Nine Worlds and from which Odhinn hanged for nine days and nights. From this "binding" to the World Tree, He was able to swoop down (into the hidden realms) and take the knowledge of the Runes. The Eihwaz rune is the stave of Self-Initiation, having the position and value of 13, runic reduction giving it the value of ᚠ + ᚦ = ᚨ (1+3 = 4).

To facilitate the altered state necessary for effective meditation/contemplation, the runer needs to be both relaxed and alert. Much time is usually wasted in trying to avoid or quieten the mind chatter at the beginning of the meditation process. The following advice and techniques have been proved to be effective for me. Try them out for yourselves. If they work for you, adopt them, if not discard them and seek others.

Light a candle and place it in line with your eye level when seated. Sit in any position that is comfortable but won't induce sleepiness, with your spine straight. Whilst focusing on the candle, commence a pattern of deep breathing. The count for this is; **breathe in while counting to 9 (nine), hold for the count of 9, breathe out to the count of 9. Repeat this till you have completed 27 full cycles of breathing**. If you find this difficult, then do at least nine full cycles ie. 3x3x9, and gradually build up the pattern by adding another three cycles at a time, at your own pace. If you cannot control your breath for these long periods, without feeling dizzy, then use a count of 3 (three) breaths ie. **In, for the count of 3, hold, for the count of 3, out, for the count of 3, hold, for the count of 3. Do this for at least 9 full cycles.** You will find your mind and body are now harmonised, relaxed and alert.

Now you are ready to start the Eihwaz contemplation. Imagine your spine being the Eihwaz rune, strong and flexible as a Yew tree. Now vibrate the sound of Eihwaz, a short sharp "i" (as in pin) This can be done initially as an external sound and internalised or begun internally. The vibration should be repetitious until you start to hear the body responding by resonating the rune as a high pitch of sound in your head. Focus your attention now on this sound. If your attention starts to waver (and it will) recommence your own vibrating until you are focused again. In this stage you are most likely to have thoughts intrude, usually of matters that are causing concern, stress or are unresolved. Do not try to resist them but acknowledge their presence and refocus on the Eihwaz vibration. They will fade away. Physical agitation as a result of these intrusions can be overcome by breathing deeply and regularly. When the internal pitch of Eihwaz becomes dominant again let your attention follow it to deeper and deeper levels. Do not allow yourself to fall into a "dreaming" state. Eventually you will attain a state of singular awareness. You are now ready to visualise the wheels with rune staves as the generator within them (see Fig.3 below).

Firstly re-visualise the Eihwaz rune (⌇) as your spinal column, now a glowing blood red colour. See a vortex of white light spinning clockwise (Deosil) entering your body at the end of your spine - the coccyx region (from below). Rist (draw) the Fehu rune (⎸) in glowing fire red. Now feel the energy permeating your total being. See the fire red colour going up your spine along the ⌇ and erupting as a fire red mist from the top of your head, surrounding your body in a cocoon of fire red light.

Next see a vortex entering your body, from the front, in the low abdominal region (corresponding to the internal reproductive organs). Rist the Thurisaz rune (⏉) in glowing purple. Now feel the energy permeating your total being. See the purple colour going down and then up your spine along the ⌇ and erupting as a purple mist from the top of your head, surrounding your body in a cocoon of purple light.

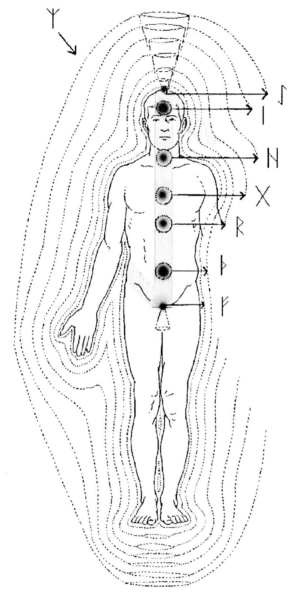

Fig. 3   **The Hvels on the Tree**

270

Next see a vortex entering your body, from the front, in the solar plexus region (corresponding to the digestive organs). Rist the Raidho rune (ᚱ) in glowing orange/red. Now feel the energy permeating your total being. See the orange/red colour going down and then up your spine along the ᛁ and erupting as an orange/red mist from the top of your head, surrounding your body in a cocoon of orange/red light.

Next see a vortex entering your body, from the front, in the sternum region (corresponding to the heart/lung organs). Rist the Gebo rune (ᚷ) in glowing orange/gold. Now feel the energy permeating your total being. See the orange/gold colour going down and then up your spine along the ᛁ and erupting as a orange/gold mist from the top of your head, surrounding your body in a cocoon of orange/gold light.

Next see a vortex entering your body, from the front, in the throat region (corresponding to the vocal organs). Rist the Hagalaz rune (ᚺ) in glowing indigo. Now feel the energy permeating your total being. See the indigo colour going down and then up your spine along the ᛁ and erupting as a indigo mist from the top of your head, surrounding your body in a cocoon of indigo light.

Next see a vortex entering your body, from the front, just above the eyebrows, in line with your nose (corresponding to the brain). Rist the Isa rune (ᛁ) in shimmering black . Now feel the energy permeating your total being. See the black colour going down and then up your spine along the ᛁ and erupting as a black mist from the top of your head, surrounding your body in a cocoon of black light.

Next see a vortex entering your body, from the top of your head, in the fontanelle region. Rist the Eihwaz rune (ᛇ) in glowing blood red. Now feel the energy permeating your total being.

See the blood red colour going down and then up your spine along the ᛋ and erupting as a blood red mist from the top of your head, surrounding your body in a cocoon of blood red light.

Lastly, visualise a cocoon of glowing white light surrounding your body. Now project your "self" identification into this glowing egg-shaped energy mass. Realise that this is your Hyde (*Hid*, OE and *Hamr*, ON) the form from which the body manifests. Rist the Elhaz rune (ᛦ) in a shimmering silver colour into this cocoon of white light. Visualise the silver colour saturating this egg-shaped glow. Now feel this composite energy permeating your total being. This is the Athem (*Aethem*, OE) energy.

Bring your consciousness back to your physical body and then your surroundings. You have now empowered your Hvels with runic energy.

Appendix
Rune Systems,
Poems and Songs.

Appendix
Other Rune Systems

In Chapter One, A Brief History of the Runes, mention was made of the Anglo-Saxon Futhark (actually Futhorc, as "a" was replaced by "o" and the "k" by "c") and the Younger Futhark. Given, below, are both these rune Systems with their Rune Names. Apply the O.E.R.Ps, given in this Appendix to the Anglo-Saxon Futhorc.

The extra nine runes, making thirty three, although having Magickal significance were not commonly used for divination. The additions came about by the dialectical and magickal confluence of the Continental Germans, Anglo-Saxons, Frisians, Jutes, Norwegians, Danes, and Celts, particuarly in Northern England and thus is outside the scope of the present work.

The O.N.R.Rhymes and the O.I.R.Poems were written specifically for the Younger Futhark (though still applicable to both the Elder and Anglo systems) being sixteen in number and were used by the Scandinavians (including the Anglo-Scandinavians) before, during and after the time of the Viking raids and settlements, ranging from Iceland to Byzantium (present day Turkey).

Read the runes (Fig.1) from left to right in the row order, top to bottom.

274

The Anglo-Saxon Futhorc:

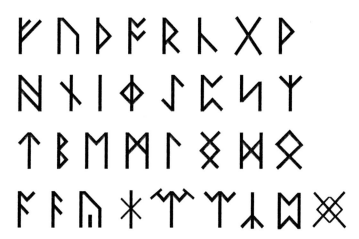

(Fig.1)

1. Feoh - wealth   2. Ur - aurochs   3. Thorn - thorn
4. Os - mouth Woden   5. Rad - riding   6. Cen - torch
7. Gyfu - giving   8. Wyn - joy

9. Haegl - hail   10. Nyd - need   11. Is - ice
12.. Ger - season   13. Eoh - yew   14. Peorth -
gaming   15. Eohl - elk   16. Sigel - sun

17. Tir - star, Tiw the god   18. Beorc - birch, poplar
19. Eh - horse   20. Man - mankind 21. Lagu - water
22. Ing - Ing the god 23. Daeg - day   24. Ethel - home

First Additions

25. Ac - oak   26. Aesc - ash 27. Yr - bow   28. Ior - beaver

Second Additions

29. Ear - earth-grave   30. Cweorth - sacred fire
31. Calc - chalice   32. Stan - stone   33. Gar - spear

The Old English Rune Poem

trans. by Daniel Bray

Wealth is a comfort to every man;
yet shall every man dole it out greatly,
if he wishes before the Lord to gain glory.

Aurochs is fierce and horned above,
a very savage beast - it fights with horns -
a well known moor-stepper; that is a bold creature!

Thorn is very sharp, for any thane
to grasp, harmful, immeasurably cruel
to any man who rests amid them.

God (Odin) is the source of all speech,
the support of wisdom and comfort of the wise
and to every earl happiness and hope.

Riding is, in the hall, for every man
easy, and very hard for him who sits upon
a powerful horse over miles of road.

Torch is by all living known for its fire,
shining and bright; it burns most often
where the nobles rest inside.

Gift for men is honour and praise,
support and worthiness; and for every exile
mercy and sustenance,
who would be otherwise destitute.

Pleasure is enjoyed by one who knows few woes,
pains and sorrows, and has himself
life and bliss and also a sufficient dwelling.

Hail is the whitest grain; it whirls from heaven's height,
it is tossed by wind storms; it is made to melt to water.

Need is oppression on the heart;
yet often it is made by men's sons
to help and to heal, however, if they heed it in time.

Ice is very cold, immeasurably slippery;
it glistens clear as glass, much like gems;
a floor wrought by frost, fair to behold.

Harvest is men's joy, when god lets,
holy heaven's king, the earth give
bright fruit to nobles and the needy.

Yew is outside an unsmooth tree,
hard and fast in the earth, fire's guard,
supported by roots, a delight on one's land.

Board-game is always play and laughter
to bold [men], where warriors sit
in the beer-hall happily together.

Elk-sedge has a home most often in the fen,
growing in water; it grimly wounds,
burning the blood of every man
who, in any way, does grasp it.

Sun by seamen is always hoped for,
when they fare far over the fishes' bath [sea],
until they the sea-steed [ship] bring to land.

Tir [Star] is a certain sign; holding trust well
with nobles; always on its course
over night-clouds; never failing.

Birch is without fruit; even so it bears
shoots without seed; its branches are beautiful,
high on its crown, fairly adorned;
loaded with leaves, touching the sky.

War-horse is, before earls, the joy of nobles,
a horse proud of hooves, when the warriors around,
wealthy in steeds, exchange speech;
and is, to the restless, ever a comfort.

Man is, in mirth, his sons' love;
each shall, though, depart from the other,
for this the Lord wills, in his judgement,
that wretched flesh be committed to the earth.

Sea is by people thought unending,
if they should venture in tossing vessel,
and them the sea-waves exceedingly frighten,
and the sea-steed does not respond to its bridle.

Ing was first among the East -Danes
seen by men, until he afterwards east
over the waves went; wagon following after;
this hardy warriors named that hero.

278

Estate is very dear to every man,
if he may there what is right and fitting
enjoy in a house most often prosperous.

Day is sent by the Lord, dear to men,
Fate's illustrious light, mirth and hope
to happy and wretched, useful to all.

Oak is on earth to the children of men
the nourishment of meat; faring often
over gannet's bath [sea] - the ocean finds
whether the oak holds nobly true.

Ash is very tall, dear to men,
unyielding on its base, holding its right place,
though many men attack it.

Yew-bow is to nobles and earls alike
joy and honour; it is fair on a steed,
steadfast on journeys, a part of war-arms.

Eel is a river-fish; and yet always takes
food on land; it has a fair dwelling
surrounded by water, where it lives in joy.

Earth is loathsome to every earl,
when steadily flesh begins
to grow cold to a corpse, to choose the earth
pale as a bedmate, fruits fall,
joys depart, vows fail.

The Younger Futhark:

The Younger Futhark had two main variations (Fig.2 a, b). These were called the "Common" or Danish and the "Short Twig" or Swedo-Norwegian. The use of either was not confined to geographical areas and both were used wherever the Scandinavians travelled or settled.

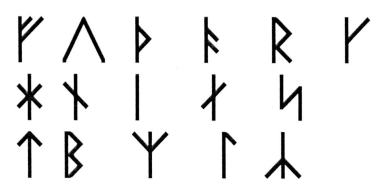

(Fig.2 a)

The Common or Danish Futhark

f	u	th	a	r	k
fe	ur	thurs	ass	reidh	kaun
wealth	drizzle	giant	god	riding	sore

h	n	i	a	s
hagall	naudh	iss	ar	sol
hail	need	ice	harvest	sun

t	b	m	l	r
tyr	bjarkan	madhr	logr	yr
tyr	birch-twig	man	water	yew

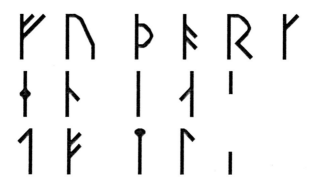

(Fig.2 b)

The Short Twig or Swedo-Norwegian

f	u	th	a	r	k
fe	ur	thurs	ass	reidh	kaun
wealth	drizzle	giant	god	riding	sore

h	n	i	a	s
hagall	naudh	iss	ar	sol
hail	need	ice	harvest	sun

t	b	m	l	r
tyr	bjarkan	madhr	logr	yr
tyr	birch-twig	man	water	yew

The Old Icelandic Rune Poem

trans. by Daniel Bray

(fe) **wealth** is kinsmen's strife/ and flood-tide's sign and grave-sorcery's way.

(ur) **drizzle** is clouds' weeping/ and the host's diminisher/ and the shepherd's hate.

(thurs) **giant** is womens' torment/and a crag-dweller/ and a giantess' husband.

(àss) **god** (Othinn) is olden-father/ and isgaro's king/ and Valhall's leader.

(reit) **riding** is a blissful sitting/and a twisting journey/ and the horse's labour.

(kaun) **sore** is child's bale/ and a battle journey/ and a house of rotten flesh.

(hagall) **hail** is a cold grain/ and a shower of sleet/ and snake-sickness (winter).

(nauth) **need** is bondswomans throe/ and a weighty choice/ and wet toilsome work.

(iss) **ice** is river-bark/ and wave-thatch/ and fated men's harm.

(àr) **harvest** is men's boon/ and a good summer/ and a ripened field.

(sol) **sun** is a shield of the clouds/ and a shining halo/ and ice's deadly sorrow.

(Tyr) **Tyr** is the one-handed god/ and the wolfs leavings/ and the temple's ruler.

(Bjarkan) **birch** is a leafy limb/ and a little tree/ and a youthful wood.

(mathr) **man** is man's game/ and increased earth/and ship's adornment.

(logr) **sea** is welling water/ and a wide cauldron/ and a plain of fish

(yr) **yew** is a bent bow/ and brittle iron/ and Fàrbauti's arrow.

The Old Norse Rune Song

trans. by Daniel Bray

(fe) **cattle** causes strife amongst kinsmen; and feeds the wolf in the woods.

(ur) **flakes** fly from bad iron; often the reindeer gallops over hard snow.

(thurs) **giants** cause women's illness; few are merry from misfortune.

(oss) **estuaries** are travelled the most when faring; but a scabbard is for swords.

(reith) **riding** is said to be worst for the horses; Reginn forged the best sword.

(kaun) **a sore** is a child s affliction; sorrow makes men pale.

(hagall) **hail** is the coldest grain; Hroptr (Othinn) shaped the world in ancient times.

(nauth) **need** makes for scant choice; the naked freeze in the frost.

(is) **ice** is called a broad bridge; the blind need to be led.

(àr) **the year** is men's profit; I say that Frodi was generous.

(sol) **the sun** is the light of the land; I bow to divine judgement.

(Tyr) **Tyr** is the one-handed god; often must a smith blow.

(bjarkan) **birch's** verdant bough; Loki brings luck from guile.

(mathr) **man** is augmented earth; mighty is the grip of the hawk.

(logr) **water** is, when falling from a mountain a force; but gold things are costly.

(yr) **yew** is an evergreen tree; and is hard when burning, to light.

I have included the 19th century German Armanen Rune System (see the chapter on A Brief History of the Runes) in this appendix (Fig.3). It is based on a personal revelation, by Guido Von List, of the '18 Rune Charms' of the *Havamal*, a section of the "Poetic Edda" (see the chapter on Magickal Applications of the Runes). For those who wish to explore this development see Flowers, S. E *The Secret of the Runes by Guido Von List*; Thorsson, E. and Hollander, L.M. in the Book Hoard.

The Armanen Futhark

Fig.3

284

The Armanen Futhark

Fa - fire generation: evolution.
Ur - the primordial: origins.
Thorr - thunderbolt: preservation.
Os - one of the æsir: speech.
Rit - the solar wheel: natural order.
Ka - Yggdrasil: the tribal tree.
Hagal - hail: introspective awareness.
Nauth - need: organic causality.
Is - ice: will power

Ar - primal fire: aryan race.
Sol - sun: victory.
Tyr - sun god: renewal.
Bar - birth: life journey.
Laf - life: cosmic law.
Ma - mothering: humanity.
Yr - bow: illusion.
Eh - marriage: continuity.
Ge - gift: awakening.

286

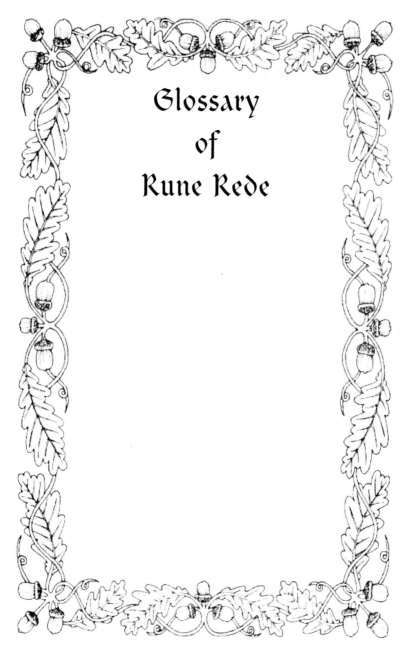

Glossary
of
Rune Rede

Rune Rede Glossary

Aegir (ON) - god of the sea who brews the god's ale drank in Asgard; husband of Ran (see Ran).

Æsir (ON) - god/esses of war, will and intelligence; of Consciousness and Wisdom. They personify self-awareness and ordered evolution. Well known are the gods Odhinn and Thorr, the goddess Frigga, and the god Loki (see listings).

Aett (ON) - (family, Aettir - plural families) a collection; a group. Specifically a group of rune staves as in the Elder Futhark: Freyja's Aett - first eight rune staves (1 to 8) of the 24 rune stave Elder Futhark; Hagal's Aett - second eight rune staves (9 to 16) of the 24 rune Elder Futhark; Tyr's Aett - third eight rune staves (17 to 24) of the 24 rune Elder Futhark

Angles - a Germanic tribe from the south eastern area of the Jutland peninsular (Denmark) who migrated to Britain in the 5th century CE.

Andvari (ON) - (careful-one) dwarf; had a secret hord of gold and precious objects stolen from the votive (sacrificial offering) areas in the river Rhine. He cursed the hord when Loki tricked him into handing it over (see Fafnir, Hreidmar, Otr).

Angrboda (ON) - (distress bidder) giantess, mother of Hella - goddess of the dead.

Archetypes - promordial images and dynamic processes of human life/consciousness including biological, psycho/bio-logical and spiritual-ideational. A Jungian term conceptually influenced by classical Greek and early Christian philosphers. Originally Jung's 'dominants of the collective unconscious'. He later stated that archetypes may be quasi-psychic in that they may originate outside of the psych, "… if archetypes were representations that originated in our consciousness (or were acquired by consciousness), we should surely understand them, and not be bewildered and atonished when they present themselves to our consciousnes" (see Collective Folk-Consciousness).

Armanen Futhark (or the Armanen Runes) - an 18-rune stave system synthesised by the German mystic Guido Von List in the late 19th century CE; still used by modern German Magicians.

Asabrù (ON) - (the bridge of the Ases) bridge of air, water and fire also called Bifrost (shimmering path) that joins the realms od Asgard and Midgard.

Ases (ME) - see Æsir.

Asgard (ON) - (enclosure of the Ases) the realm where dwell the Aesiric god/esses; on the highest metaphysical plane. It is written that in Asgard there are twelve divine gods and twelve divine goddesses (see Vanaheim and Lossalfheim).

Ask (ME) - (Askr ON) the first man and Embla (ON) the first woman shaped from two fallen trees found on the seashore - man from the Ash tree, woman from the Elm tree. Odhinn breathed the life-spirit into them; Vili gave them wits and feelings; Vè gave them senses - hearing and sight.

Asynjur (ON) - goddesses, feminine plural of Æsir.

Athem (Aethem OE) - animating and unifying principle that links the body with its non-material aspects; holds the Ferth to the body (Lyke); the "cord" that binds body and soul during life and keeps connection while the Hyde (subtle body) is faring forth to other worlds (see Ferth, Hyde, Lyke).

Audumla (ON) - (fecund care?) Primal Cow formed from the ice thaw in the Ginnungagap (beguiling void). She fed the frost-giant Ymir from her four teats and shaped Buri, Odhinn's grandfather by licking the salty ice blocks (see Ymir).

Aurochs; Aurochse (German) - great and fierce wild oxen or bison, now extinct, which once inhabited the vast plains and woodlands of Europe; could not be domesticated but were hunted for their flesh, hide and horns.

Asvithr or Alsvinn (ON) - (all swift) a giant who was given runes for the Etins' use.

Axis - (central) of the Multiverse is known as the World Tree and is called Yggdrasil (Ygg's Horse, ie. Odhinn's Steed), Irminsul (Primal Pillar) and Làradr (Counsel Giver). Its roots rest in the tri-level Well of Wyrd (the container of all activity) which brings forth all manifestation in the Nine Worlds (see listings).

Baldur (ON) - (bold) god of youth, hope and courage; son of Odhinn and Frigga, husband of Nanna (mamma?); one of the Æsir, he will inherit his father's throne as chief of the gods after Ragnarok.

Baugi (ON) - (bowed) a giant; Suttung's brother (see Bolverkr, Suttung).

Bifrost (ON) - see Asabrù.

Bor (ON) - (son?) the son of Buri (son?) and Bestla (bark?) who was the daughter of Bolthor (evil thorn).

Bolverkr (ON) - (evil doer) Odhinn in disguise tricked Suttung's brother Baugi into drilling a hole in the base of the mountain Hnitborg. He turned himself into a snake and entered to steal the Mead of Inspiration (see Gunnlod, Kvasir, Hnitborg, Mead of Inspiration).

Breidablik (ON) - (broad shining) Dwelling Hall of the god Baldur (see Baldur).

Brisingamen (ON) - (necklace of the Brisings', flaming necklace), made by four dwarfs, given to Freyja for having sex with each in turn. These four dwarfs were personifications of the four directions - North, South, East and West. The possession of the necklace gave her power over the earth-elements and associated spirits (see Freyja, Dwarfs).

Celts - an Indo-European people who spread across Europe and Asia Minor before the Germanic migrations; contemporary with and closely related to the Germanics, ethnically and culturally. Dominant inhabitants of the British Isles at the time of the Germanic migrations.

Cisa or Zisa - (goddess; earth-mother?) feminine twin of Tyr (see Tyr).

Collective Folk-Consciousness - "collective unconscious" - portion of our psyche that is common. Jungian psychological concept; genetic and/or psychic repository of racial memory- a reality construct (see Archetypes).

Dainn (ON) - (dead) an elf who was given runes for the Elves' use (see Álfheim).

Deosil - the clockwise direction - from left to right.

Disir (ON); - ancestral feminine guardian spirits of individuals, families and tribes.

Divination - the act of divining, a prophecy, a prediction; inspired guesswork.

Draugar (ME) - (Draugr ON) the 'undead'; the animated corpse of one whose Athem has not completely severed from the Hyde. They are usually dangerous to the living.

Dwarfs - Also called Dark Elves; a race of beings shaped from the maggots that infested the remains of the primal frost-giant Ymir. Said to dwell in the mountains, grottos and under-ground caverns. They are shrewd beings and excellent smiths, shapers of power and form - emotions and matter -

who produce items of wondrous magick that the gods covet and sometimes gain. Their leader is Modsognir (frenzy roarer) and his deputy is Durinn (sleepy).

Dvalinn (ON) - (dawdler) a dwarf who was given runes for the Dwarves' use.

Elder Futhark - a magickal system of symbols consisting of 24 rune staves. The word Futhark comes from the sound representation of the first six staves: F,U,Th,A,R,K, much in the same way as the word "alphabet" comes from the sound of the first two letters of the Greek alphabet: Alpha and Beta. Origin between 200BCE and 200 CE.

Elements - forces of numinous reality that constitute the cosmos - Fire, Air, Water, Ice, Earth, Iron, Yeast, Salt, Venom.

Elves (Light) - (Alfs ON) they dwell in Lossàlfheim (Light Elf Home), and are the shapers of thought and matter and warders of the natural world. The Light Elves give their allegiance to the god Freyr who received their kingdom as a "Tooth Gift" from the Æsir.

Elvidnir (ON) - (misery) Dwelling Hall of the goddess Hella (see Hella).

Embla (ON) - the first woman shaped from the Elm tree (see Ask)

Etins (ME, Eoten OE) - or Jotnar (ON plural of Jotun) are giant preconscious beings whose function is the dissolution of form in nature which is necessary for new form to arise. Thurses (ME) Thursar (ON) and Risar (ON) are other names given to the same race; dwelling place is Jotunheim (see listings).

Fafnir (ON) - (embracer) son of Hreimar, brother of Otr; became a dragon when he in turn came into possession of Andvari's horde (see Andvari, Hreidmar, Loki, Otr).

Fenrir (ON) - (fen dweller) the mighty wolf, child of Loki, who will slay the god Odhinn in the final battle called Ragnarok (destruction of the powers); see Loki.

Fensalir (ON) - (marsh halls) Dwelling Hall of the goddess Frigga (see Frigga).

Ferth (ME) - (Feorh OE) is all the non-physical components of the psycho-somatic complex, excluding the Fetch, that survive the death of the body; "the self".

Fetch (ME) - (Faecce OE; Fylgja ON) the bridging consciousness that ties the personal component to the ancestral component; a semi-independent being attached to the soul during the lifetime of the body; a recorder of all deeds; a guardian.

Fiolkyngi (ON) - (great cunning/wisdom of the folk) magick; (see Seidhr, Seith).

Fjalarr (ON) - (deceiver) one of two dwarfs who and Galarr (screamer) were envious of Kvasir's wisdom and the attention he attracted so they slew him and magickally brewed his blood into mead (see Galarr, Kvasir).

Fjorgvin (ON) - see Jord; Nerthus.

Folkvang (ON) - Field of the Warrior-Folk; Freyja's hall reserved for the valiant warriors who love the earth and wish to be rebirthed back into their family; (see Freyja).

Forsetti (ON) - (reconciler of deeds) god of law-giving, settler of law suits and quarrels. Patron god of the Frisians [the Germanic people who inhabited the Netherlands/Holland]. Son of Baldur and his wife Nanna (mamma?); one of the Æsir.

Freki (ON) - (rapaciousness) see Geri.

Freyja (ON) - (lady) goddess of love and war, riches and strife; sister of Freyr, daughter of Jord and Njord; has first choice of

293

all slain warriors in battle; leader of the Valkyries; possessor of the Brisingamen; mistress of Seidr Magick which she taught to Odhinn. She is one of the Vanir (see Brisingamen; Odhinn, Seidr, Valkyries).

Freyr (ON) - (lord) god of fecundity and nature, who received the kingdom of Álfheim as a "Tooth Gift" from the Æsir; brother of Freyja, son of Jord and Njord; called upon for frith (fruitful peace at home) and is often pictured with an enlarged phallus. He is also a deity of love and pleasure. He is also a warrior-god and is called upon for protection in battle; Lord of the Elves and is especially connected with the worship given to ancestral spirits and the spirits of nature. He is one of the Vanir (see Ing).

Frigga (ON) - (lady) goddess of silent wisdom, duty and feminine mysteries; known as the "silent seeress"; aka Hlìn (protectress), she is the Great Mother; wife of Odhinn and mother of Baldur; patron goddess of the home and married women's mysteries including traditional crafts (spinning, weaving, cooking, sewing) and associated magick. She is called on for protection of women in childbirth and to protect children, especially sons going to war. She is one of the Æsir (see Saga).

Frisians - a Germanic tribe from north western area of the Netherlands, Belgium and Germany who migrated to Britain in the 5th century CE.

Frost Giants - primal entities of Ice who were spawned from the sweat of the first Frost-giant Ymir (see Audumla, Ymir).

Fulla (ON) - (abundance) handmaiden of the goddess Frigga (see Frigga).

Futhorc - the Anglo-Saxon (or Anglo-Frisian) rune system consisting of a total of first 24, then 29 and finally 33 rune staves.

Fylgjur (ON) - Plural of Fylgja; (see Fetch).

Galarr (ON) - (screamer) one of two dwarfs who were envious of Kvasir's wisdom and the attention he attracted so they slew him and magickally brewed his blood into mead (see Fjalarr, Kvasir).

Galdr (ON) or Galdar - (singing) form of magick; involves the directing of runic energy through chanting, visualising and risting runes by the intention - the will power alone - of the magician.

Garm (ON) - (rag) hound-dog, guardian of Nàgrind (corpse gate) the gateway to Hel; animal Fetch (familiar) of Hella (see Fetch, Hel, Hella, Nàgrind).

Gerd (ON) - (fenced-in) a giantess, wife of Freyr (see Freyr, Skirnir)

Geri (ON) - (greed) and Freki (ON) (rapaciousness), twin wolves who guard Odhinn's High Seat; the wolves of war.

Ghost (ME) - (Gàst OE) a disembodied spirit but also the spirit within a living body. (see Ferth).

Ginnungagap (ON) - (beguiling void) the primal void where fire and ice came into contact forming all life.

Gjallabrù (ON) - (resounding bridge) a bridge connecting Hel and Asgard.

Gjollarhorn (ON) - (resounding horn) blown by Heimdall at the time of Ragnarok to warn the gods of the approaching danger and call them to battle.

Gladsheim (ON) - (home of gladness) Dwelling Hall of the god Odhinn (see Odhinn).

Gleipnir (ON) - (open one) magickal fetter name made by the dwarfs to bind the wolf Fenrir.

Glitnir (ON) - (glistening) Dwelling Hall of the god Forsetti (see Forsetti).

Gna (ON) - (plenty?) a messenger and handmaiden of the goddess Frigga (see Frigga).

Godhar (ON) - collective plural for the heathen priesthood ie. priests and priestesses.

Godhi (ON) - heathen priest.

Goths (Greek) - (the Gothic people- from *Gutthiuda*) one of an ancient Teutonic race that originated in Scandinavia. The settled in the area between the rivers Elbe and Vistula before dividing into two groups, the Ostrogoths (east) and Visigoths (west). The eastern tribes travelled and settled throughout Eurasia while the western tribes remained in Europe, eventually overrunning the Roman Empire before the end of the 5th century CE.

Grid (ON) - (greed) a giant; mother of the god Vìdar (see Vìdar).

Gullinborsti (ON) - (golden-bristles) a Boar magically fashioned by the dwarfs for Freyr; his Fetch (see Fetch).

Gungnir (ON) - (swaying one) Odhinn's spear which was described as strong and slender and always found its mark when cast (see Ivaldi's sons).

Gunnlod (ON) - (war summons) a giant; daughter of Suttung who guarded the Mead of Inspiration; seduced by Bolverkr (Odhinn in disguise) who stole the mead by drinking the three cauldrons (see Bolverkr, Hnitborg, Mead of Inspiration).

Gydhja (ON) - or Gythja, heathen priestess.

Hallingskidi (ON) - (asymetrically horned), another name of Heimdall, associated with the Ram (See Heimdall, Rig).

Hamingja (ON) - Luck, see Main and Speed.

Hati (ON) - (destroyer) a wolf-shaped troll that pursues Mani, the Moon god's horse and wagon; will devour the moon at Ragnarok (see Ragnarok).

Havamal (ON) - (sayings of Har - the high one) part of the Icelandic text called the Poetic Edda.

Hel (ON) - (concealed) on the lowest metaphysical plane; realm of the dead which is not a place of eternal punishment but a place of rest for souls awaiting their rebirths into Midgard. Many of its halls are bright and warm where existence is not much different from Midgard.

Hella (ON) - the goddess of the dead, specifically those who perish from illness or old age; said to be half beautiful and half rotting corpse; daughter of the giantess Angrboda (distress bidder) by Loki who has the ability to change sex and /or be hermaphroditic); sister of the wolf Fenrir (fen dweller) who devours Odhinn at Ragnarok (destruction of the powers) and the Midgard-Serpent Jormungand (mighty wand) who encircles the earth biting his own tail.

Helvegr (ON) - (hellway) the road between Asgard and Hel.

Heimdall (ON) - (home brightener); aka Vindlher (watchman), guardian of the three stranded (air, fire and water) Rainbow bridge between Midgard (Earth) and Asgard (Heaven) called Bifrost (shimmering path). The protector of those seeking higher consciousness; one of the Æsir.

Heruli - a Germanic tribe originally from southern Sweden who followed the migratory path of the Goths into the Ukraine then into central Europe, France and overan Italy in 476 CE; then served as mercenaries in the armies of the (Roman) Western Empire. No record after 557CE.

High (ME) - (Hyge OE) the intellect and includes analytical prowess and wilfulness. Its components are: The Angit (OE) - the five senses which collect information; The Sefa (OE) - reason and thought, the power of reckoning;

The Wit (OE) - memory selection and retrieval.

Hildisvini (ON) - (battle-swine) Freyja's animal Fetch (familiar); a magickal Sow made by the Dwarfs.

Hlesey (ON) - (sea island) Dwelling Hall of the god/esses Aegir and Ran.

Hlidskjalf (ON) - (gate-tower?) Odhinn's High Seat in Asgard from which he can view all the Nine Worlds. He sees all happenings, and hears all from his two ravens - Huginn (thought) and Muninn (memory) - who travel throughout the Nine Worlds and report back to him every day. His throne is protected by the twin wolves Geri (greed) and Freki (rapaciousness).

Himminbjorg (ON) - (heaven mountain) Hall Dwelling of the god Heimdall (see Heimdall).

Hnitborg (ON) - (crashing rock) mountain home of Suttung and Gunnlod within Jotunheim; holding place of the Mead of Inspiration (see Suttung, Gunnlod).

Hoenir (ON) - (self?) Odhinn's taciturn brother (see Mimir).

Hodur (ON) - (warrior) blind brother of Baldur whom he slew with a mistletoe twig given to him by Loki.

Hreidmar (ON) - (frightener?) father of the shape-shifter Otr (otter) and Fafnir. Otr was brother to Fafnir (embracer) who became a dragon when he in turn came into possession of Andvari's horde (see Otr).

Hrimfaxi (ON) - (ice-mane) Mani the Moon god's horse; is pursued by the troll-wolf Hati from the place called Jarnvidr (iron wood) in Jotunheim (home of the giants). Hati will

298

devour Hrimfaxi, and the moon, at Ragnarok

Huginn (ON) - (thought) and Muninn (ON) (memory); twin Ravens who travel throughout the Nine Worlds reporting back to Odhinn everday on what they have observed; Odhinn's Fetches (see Fetch).

Hyde (ME) - (Hìd OE; Hamr ON) the shape or form, a subtle energy vehicle that has the approximate shape of the physical body; the "skin of the soul". It carries the Ferth when faring forth in life and after death.

Idavoll (ON) - (place of splendour) Dwelling Hall of the goddess Idunna (see Idunna).

Idesa (OS) - see Disir.

Idunna (ON) - (rejuvenator) goddess of spring; She is of a race of gods even older than the Vanir (fertility gods) and personifies the essence of the female principle, just as the god Ing-Freyr personifies the male principle. Daughter of Ivaldi, aunt of Ullur and sister of Nanna (Baldur's wife) and Orvandil; wife of Bragi (Poetry). Idunna is the custodian of the golden apples that the Æsir gods consume to maintain their eternal youth.

Indo-European - designation of the ethnic culture and/or language group that formed in Europe about 11,000 years ago, known as the Caucasian, Aryan or Indo-Iranian race. Spread throughout Europe and Asia-Minor 5000-4000 years ago.

Ing (ON) - another name for Freyr; he mysteriously appeared, from the west, in the land of the Angles in Denmark. He brought peace, harmony and plenty to the land. He sired a line of rulers and then just as mysteriously disappeared. Ing-Freyr (a.k.a Ingvi-Freyr) personifies the male principle of immortality through rebirth (see Angles, Freyr).

Irminsul (OS) - (primal pillar)the Saxon name for the cosmological World Tree - the central axis of the Nine Worlds (see Yggdrasil).

Ivaldi's sons - dwarf smiths who magically fashioned a wig of gold for Sif; a ship named Skidbladnir (wooden bladed) for Freyr; and a spear for Odhinn named Gungnir (swaying one).

Jarnvidr (ON) - (iron wood) a vast forest, here lurks the mighty wolf Fenrir (fen dweller).

Jord (ON); Nerthus (F) - (earth) mother earth goddess, twin of Njord, mother of the twins Freyr and Freyja; She is one of the Vanir.

Jormungand (ON) - (mighty wand) the terrible serpent who dwells within the ocean that encircles Midgard; He is so long that he bites on his own tail; He devours Thorr at Ragnarok (see Loki).

Jotnar (ON plural of Jotun) - giants (see Etins; Thurs).

Jotunheim (ON (the home of the Giants) on the second highest metaphysical plane (see Etins; Thurs).

Jutes - a Germanic tribe from western and south Jutland (Denmark) who migrated to Britain in the 5th century CE.

Kvasir (ON) - (wise one?) a magickal being shaped from the spittle of the Æsir and Vanir gods (see Bolverkr).

Kvollheimr (ON) - ('home of twilight') a hall of punishment for the wicked in Hel (see Hel. Niflhel).

Làradr, Laeradr (ON) - (counsel giver) another name for the World Tree; the centrtal axis of the Nine Worlds (see World Tree).

Landvættir (ON) - land spirits, guardians of natural places.

Landvidi (ON) - (forest land) Dwelling Hall of the god Vìdar (see Vìdar).

Lìfthràsir (ON) - Leifthrasir (thriving remnant) a man who will hide in the World Tree (Yggdrasil) to survive the holocaust of Ragnarok.

Lìf (ON) - (life) a woman who will hide in the World Tree (Yggdrasil) to survive the holocaust of Ragnarok.

Loki (ON) - a trickster god, blood-brother (and shadow side) of Odhinn, father of Fenrir, Hella and Jormungard. He joins forces with Surt at the time of Ragnarok.

Lossàlfheimr (ON) - (Light Elf Home) in the highest metaphysical realm but easily accessible from Midgard (see Elves).

Lyfjaberg (ON) - (hill of living) Dwelling Hall of the Goddess Jord (see Jord, Nerthus).

Lyke (ME) - (Lìc OE) the body; the vehicle through which we work our will and gain experience by the effects of its action.

Main (ME) - (Maegen OE) personal power (see Speed).

Mani (ON) - (the Man-in-the-Moon); the moon personified, the son of Mundilfari (turner?); he drives the chariot carrying the physical moon across the night sky; brother of the sun goddess Sunna (see Sunna).

Mead of Inspiration - brewed from the blood of Kvasir; kept by Suttung in three vessels called Odroerir (frenzy stirrer), Bodn (vessel) and Son (blood); see Fjalarr, Galarr, Gunlodd, Kvasir, Suttung.

Meed (ME) - (Maed OE) reward or credit; skuld for right actions (see Skuld).

Midgard (ON) - (middle enclosure) the second highest metaphysical realm; the middle level inhabited by humanity.

Mimir (ON) - (mindful or memory wise); brother of Odhinn's Etin-mother Bestla (bark?); was a peace hostage to the Vanir along with Odhinn's taciturn brother Hoenir. When they discovered that Hoenir (self?) could not act without the advice of Mimir (mind?), they decapitated Mimir and sent his head back to Odhinn (inspiration). Odhinn preserved the head with herbs and spells and consults the disembodied Mimir for advice. His head rests besides one of the wells under the roots of the World-Tree (see Mimir's Well, Well of Wyrd, Irminsul, Nine Worlds, World Tree, Yggdrasil).

Mimir's Well - (Mimisbrunn ON) - (well of mindfulness) Dwelling Hall of the Etin Mimir; second deepest level of the Well of Wyrd; receptacle of ancestral wisdom; Odhinn sacrificed an eye into the well to gain wisdom (see Well of Wyrd).

Mind (ME) - (Mynd OE) cognitive consciousness; contains personal memories of deeds, knowledge and wisdom (OE Myne) along with ancestral memories and inherited instinct (OE Orthanc). The ancestral memories are of actual deeds, lessons learned and errors made - the collective (folk) unconscious (see listing and Archetypes).

Mjollnir (ON) - a magickal hammer; weapon owned by the god Thorr; always finds its mark and returns to Thorr's hand when thrown; generates lightening and thunder; made by the dwarfs (see Thorr, Sif).

Mood (ME) - (Mòd OE) seat of all emotions both simple and complex and is closely linked with the Wode.

Multiverse - see the Nine Worlds,

Mundilfari (ON) - (turner?) see Mani.

Muninn (ON) - (memory); see Huginn.

Muspellheim (ON) - (home of doom?) on the lowest metaphysical plane; a region of pure fire (possibly anti-matter?).

Muspell, sons of - dwellers of Muspellheim. Their ruler is the fire-being Surt (black-one) who will lead the attack on the Æsir and Vanir at the time of Ragnarok.

Myrkvidhr (ON) - (murk wood) a vast forest separating Muspellheim from Asgard.

Nàgrind (ON) - (corpse gate) the gate at Hel's entrance that separates the land of the living from the dead.

Narvi (ON) - (narrow?) [Narfi?]son of Loki slain by his brother Vàli (foreign?) after Thorr and other gods changed him into a wolf; his entrails are Loki's bonds (see Sigyn).

Nàstrandir (ON) - (shore of corpses) deeper hall of Hel; reserved for evil doers who passed through Hel to die a second death by the dragon called Nidhogg (vicious blow) who also chews on the roots of the World Tree -Yggdrasil (see Niflhel).

Nerthus (F) - see Jord.

Niflheim (ON) - (mist home) on the lowest metaphysical plane; the land of the dead, of the souls unworthy to enter Asgard. It is another aspect of Hel; described as a place of bitter cold, mist and unending night - ice and darkness.

Niflhel (ON) - (concealed mist) the lowest metaphysical plane; where the souls that are too evil to dwell in the halls of the goddess of the dead - Hella (concealer) - pass down into the final darkness to die a second death into oblivion.

Nidhogg (ON) - (vicious blow) a serpent who consumes the subtle bodies of those in Niflhel. This same serpent gnaws on the roots of the World Tree.

Nine Noble Virtues - the Germanic Heathen ethical code; Courage, Truth, Honour, Fidelity, Hospitality, Discipline, Industriousness, Self-Reliance and Perseverance.

Nine Worlds, The - a three tiered system of cosmology with each tier consisting of three worlds with all being supported and penetrated by a central axis (the World Tree); these worlds though separate in time and space essentially co-exist unilaterally, collectively called the Multiverse.

Noatun (ON) - (harbour) Dwelling Hall of the god Njord (see Njord).

Nott (ON) - (night) mother of Jord.

Njord (ON) - (earth enjoyer) god of wealth/waterways, cargos/ ships. He is the twin of Jord, the father of the twins Freyja and Freyr; He is one of the Vanir.

Norns (ME) - also known as the "Wyrd Sisters"; Primal beings who are the personifications of the cosmic law (orlog). Their names, in ON, are Urdhr - "That which has become", Verdhandi - "That which is becoming" and Skuld - "That which shall (is obliged to) come"

Odhinn (ON) - (inspirer, frenzy) Odin, Oden, Woden, Wotan; the one-eyed god of magick, secret wisdom and death; archetypical magician, shape-shifter and shaman - giver of the Runes. He is also the god of poetry and intellectual insight. He can inspire either enlightenment or madness (see Mimir's Well, Valkyries).

Odhinn's Steed - Yggdrasil, Ygg meaning "terrible" (a name of Odhinn); another name for the World Tree.

Old English Rune Poems - oral collection of runic poems; one for each 29 staves of the first revised Anglo-Saxon (or Anglo-Frisian) Futhorc, recorded by Christian monks up to the 11th century CE.

Old Icelandic Rune Poems - oral collection of runic poems from Iceland; one for each of the 16 staves of the Younger Futhark recorded by Christian monks in the 12th Century CE.

Old Norse Rune Songs - oral collection of runic poems from Norway; one for each of the 16 staves of the Younger Futhark recorded by Christian monks in the 12th Century CE.

Orlaw (OE) - (Orlog ON) the primal layers of events (which becomes the governing law) to ensure the unfolding of events to come, ie.the Wyrd.

Orvandil (ON) - (high apart?) a star being; sister of Idunna and father of Ullur (see Ullur).

Otr (ON) - (otter) a shape-shifter, son of Hreidmar and brother of Fanir (embracer); Loki had mistaken Otr for an animal and slain for his beautiful hide (see Andvari, Fafnir, Loki, Hreidmar).

Ragnarok (ON) - (destruction of the powers) the final conflict between order and chaos that will see the Nine Worlds destroyed (but not the World Tree). The Æsir and Vanir with the help of the Einherjar fight the Sons of Muspell who join with Loki, his spawn and the restless dead to battle to the death on the Idavoll plain; the end of the present epoch of the Multiverse.

Ran (ON) - (plunder) 'Mother of the Waves'; She is wife of the god Aegir (sea); held responsible for the drowning (called 'Ran's embrace') of people during storms at sea. She has nine daughters (waves) who cause distress to unwary ships enabling Ran to casts her 'golden net' over sailors, dragging them down to her domain.

Ratatosk (ON) - the squirrel which runs up and down Yggdrasil exchanging taunts between the Eagle at its crown and the serpent (Nidhogg) at its roots (see World Tree).

Rig (ON - possibly of Celtic origin?) - (king) Heimdall as the progenitor and instructor of the three classes of people in society - servants, freeman and rulers; god of intellect, learning, teaching. He taught Odhinn's Runes to mankind.

Risar (ON) - giants (see Etin, Thurs, Jotnar).

Risting (ME) - (Rìsta ON) act of cutting, carving or sawing especially used in relation to the runes.

Runa (Gothic) - see Rûne.

Rûne (OE); Rùne (ON) - mystery, secret, whisper or roar of power; an incantation, magickal binding; a written/inscribed character representing/invoking symbolic meaning.

Runer (ME) - one who engages in the study of rune lore and the practice of rune craft.

Runic Code - a system of numerological values and correspondences applied to the rune staves within the Elder Futhark.

Rune Lore - history, knowledge and wisdom pertaining to the runes.

Rune Master - one who has mastered the understanding and application of the runes.

Saga (ON) - (history) goddess of time and events, recall and memory. She is the patron of writers and story-tellers; one of the Asynjur (æsir goddess), the daughter of Odhinn and Frigga; may be an aspect of Frigga; Saga sings the songs and chants the ancestral stories in the company of Odhinn (see Frigga).

Saxons - a Germanic tribe from the border region of southern Jutland (Denmark) and north western Germany who migrated to Britain in the 5th century CE.

Seidhr (ON) - (Seith) meaning 'to seethe', a form of folk magick akin to Shamanism practiced by the Germanic peoples (see Seith).

Seith (ME) - (seething) also known as Fiolkyngi (great

cunning/wisdom of the folk) and involves the spell chanting, rune risting, visualisation and the evocation of external entities god/esses and/or spirits to achieve the desired result. The practice of Spae (scrying - clairvoyance); prediction of Orlog and out-of-body journeying (faring forth) is a part of Seith. This magick is of an elemental kind having to do with understanding and manipulating natural phenomena (see Seidhr).

Shamanism - magico-religious practice of tribal communities; involves trance states, out - of - body experiences, communication with spirit world. Used for healing, divination and magick.

Shild (ME) - (Scyld OE; Skuld ON) debt or obligation for wrong actions.

Sif (ON) - (relation) fertility goddess best known for her long rippling golden hair which was likened to ripe grain swaying in the breeze; mother of the winter archer-god Ullur and wife of the god Thorr.

Sigil - a symbolic ideograph, eg.the Valknut.

Sigyn (ON) - (victory friend) Loki's wife; holds a bowl above his face to catch serpent venom that drips on him while he lays bound until Ragnarok (see Loki).

Skadi (ON) - (harm) protective goddess of the mountains; goddess of winter, revenge, hunting, skiing. Patroness of female warriors; short-time husband to Njord who selected him as her husband in compensation for her father Thjazi (self-serving) who was slain by Thorr.

Skidbladnir (ON) - (wooden bladed) Freyr's ship which was large enough to carry all the gods into battle at Ragnarok but could be folded up like a cloth and carried in a purse (see Ivaldi's sons).

Skinfaxi (ON) - (shining mane) horse of the goddess Sunna (see Sunna).

Skirnir (ON) - (bright-one) servant of Freyr sent to Gerd with his sword and horse, as wooing gifts to gain her hand in marriage.

Skoll (ON) - (treachery) a wolf-shaped troll (magical being) which pursues the Sun and will devour in at Ragnarok.

Skuld (ON) - see Shild.

Sleipnir (ON) - (slipper) Odhinn's eight-legged horse riden in his function of Psychopomp (guide to souls of the dead); and to travel throughtout the Nine Worlds.

Sokkvabekk (ON) - (sunken bench) Dwelling Hall of the goddess Saga (see Saga).

Soul (ME) - (Sawol OE) in heathen lore referred to the mortal aspects of the psycho-somatic complex - those that perished with the body. The three main categories of the soul (as in the present day meaning of "immortal spirit") are the Mind, the Memory and the Emotions.

Spækona (ON) - feminine; a seeress, prophetess.

Spæmadhr (ON) - masculine; a seer, prophet.

Speed (ME) - (Spaed OE) luck or power of the individual and has the same meaning as the Old Norse term Hamingja and was believed to be tied to the Fetch and determined by the Orlog. It was passed down through families or transferred to individuals by willing intent/magick.

Staves - (glyphs, characters and/or the wood its risted on); another name for a rune symbol which were used to represent or invoke each secret/mystery. They embodied the esoteric law attached to each symbol.

Sumbel (or Symbel) - prechristian Norman dialect ?, derived

308

from Assembly (Fr); ritual drinking, toasting and recitation as a sacred rite.

Sunna (ON) - (a.k.a Sol by the Vikings) who personifies the Sun; charioteer of that heavenly body; said to be the manifested (material) eye of Odhinn (see Mani); a.k.a Alfrodul (elf-beam) and alludes to her connection with the realm of the Light-Elves

Surt (ON) - see Muspell, sons of; Ragnarok.

Suttung (ON) - (sup-heavy) a giant; claimed the mead brewed from Kvasir's blood by the dwarfs Fjalarr and Galarr as compensation for the murder of his parents by this evil pair but boasted to all and sundry of his magickal brew (see Fjalarr, Gjalarr, Kvasir).

Svartàlfheim (ON) - (home of the Dark Elves) on the second highest metaphysical plane (see Dwarfs).

Symbel - see Sumbel.

Tacitus - 1st century CE Roman Historian who studied the Germanic peoples.

Thjazi (ON) - (self-serving?) a giant; father of the goddess Skadi (harm) who, disguised as an eagle, kidnapped Idunna to gain possession of the apples of eternal youth (see Skadi, Idunna).

Thorr (ON) - (giant) a.k.a Asa-Thorr and 'old redbeard'; god of fertility and generation, Defender of the Realm of the Gods (Asgard) and the Mankind (Midgard); enemy of the giants. Son of Odhinn and Jord; husband of Sif. Has a magickal hammer called Mjollnir He is one of the Æsir (see Mjollnir, Sif, Thjazi).

Thrudvang (ON) - (field of strength) Dwellin Hall of the god Thorr (see Thorr).

Thrymheim (ON) - (home of noise) Dwelling Hall of the goddess Skadi (see Skadi).

Thurs (ON) - (giant), Thursar (plural), Thurses (ME); a race of huge preconscious beings who personify the chaotic forces of destruction in nature necessary for new (ordered) forms to arise (see Etins).

Troll (ON) - a magickal being of the Thurs race and/or of the land spirits known as Landvættir (see Etins, Thurs).

True Will - our deepest spiritual yearnings emerging from the Wòd which are a source of power; spiritual potential.

Tyr (ON) - (heavenly or god) Germanic equivalent of the Indo-European "Sky-Father"; warrior god of justice (and necessary sacrifice) and is associated with the "Thing" (law council); a.k.a "One-handed" because he sacrificed his hand in the mouth of the Fenris Wolf to aid in Fenrir's binding by the Æsir gods (see Fenrir, Loki).

Ullur (ON) - (brilliant one or glorious); archer god; god of winter, patron of hunters and single combatants, skiers and skaters. Son of the star-being Orvandil (high apart?) and Sif, Thorr's wife, stepson to Thorr. Also nephew to Idunna (goddess of spring) and Baldur's wife Nanna (mamma?)

Valgrind (ON) - gate of the slain or chosen; an ideographic sigil that enables or expands consciousness; see below.

Valholl (ON) - Hall of the Slain or Chosen; Odhinn's hall in Asgard reserved for the valiant warriors who die in battle and/or those who will join him to fight in the final batltle of Ragnarok.

Vàli (ON) - (foreign?) brother of Narvi [Narfi?] whom he slew; son of **Loki** (see Narvi, Sygin).

Valknut (ON) - knot of the slain or chosen; an ideographic sigil that binds or limits consciousness; same form as Valgrind but different purpose .

Valkyries (ME) - 'choosers of the slain'; (ON Valkyrjur, feminine plural) supernatural feminine beings in Odhinn's and Freyja's service who choose the warriors to die in battle. Their souls are then escorted either to Freyja's Hall - Folkvang or to Odhinn's Hall - Valholl; also act as serving maids at the table to these heroes called Einherjar (lone fighters). They act as guardians in battle to protect certain chosen ones destined to serve a high purpose in life (see Folkwang; Valholl).

Valkyrja (ON) - singular feminine; 'chooser of the slain' (see above).

Vanaheim (ON) - (home of hope) Dwelling Hall of the Vanir. In the highest metaphysical realm (see Vanir).

Vanatroth (ME) - (Vanatru ON) worship of the Vanir; those who are true to the Vanir deities (see Vanir).

Vanir (ON) - (Wanes ME) god/esses of nature and instinct, of fertility and material plenty.

Vathrudnir (ON) - (mighty weaver) a giant. During an exchange the reveals to Odhinn that he is able to read the runes of the giants and of the gods because he has visited all the worlds including the land of the dead.

Vafthrudnismal (ON) - (sayings of Vathrudnir); part of the Poetic Edda', text from Iceland.

Vè (ON) - (self contained) a triunal aspect of the god Odhinn who gave the first man and woman (Ask and Embla) their senses - hearing and sight.

Vè (ON) - (sacred enclosure) an area set aside as a sanctuary for religious and magickal use; an area dedicated to the god/esses; hallowed ground, a Banner (signifying separation).

Velsofa (ON) - (sleep ease) Dwelling Hall of god Mani (see Mani).

Vidar (ON) - (wide provider) god of woodlands; son of Odhinn, his mother Grid (greed) is of the Thurs (giant) race; strongest god after Thorr. He is one of the Æsir.

Vili (ON) - (will) a triunal aspect of the god Odhinn who gave the the first man and woman (Ask and Embla) their wits and feelings.

Vindvefja (ON) - (wind weaver) Dwelling Hall of the goddess Sunna (see Sunna).

Vitka (ON) - feminine; sorcereress, witch, shamana, magician.

Vitki (ON) - masculine; sorcerer, warlock, shaman, magician.

Vœlva (ON) - a woman with prophetic talents who also has other "magical" skills (see Seidr, Seith).

Web of Wyrd - connecting force linking the World Tree with the Nine Worlds; reaches in all directions through out the Multiverse; a state of consciousness binding all realities, both actual and potential.

Well of Wyrd - (Urdarbrunn ON) container of all events - it structures and contains time in the Nine Worlds; has three levels. Actions having a far reaching effect that impact on the flow of time settle into the deepest level of the Well of Wyrd. Those of lesser significance fall into the second level known as the Well of Mimir (mindfulness). Those of the least importance drop into the third level known as the Well of Hvergelmir (seething kettle). Collectively they bring forth all manifestation in the Nine Worlds; wardered by the Norns (see Norns).

Wicca (OE) - Wicce (OE) male/female witch (see Vitki, Vitka).

Wihstead (OE) - a sacred enclosure; see Vè.

Will (ME) - (Willa OE) force of self-determination; it allows the harnessing of the thoughts from the Wode to be transformed into deeds. It can summon Wode (inspiration) and also Main (power) from hidden or runic (secret) places; part of the Ferth.

Wode (ME) - (Wòd OE) seat of inspiration/frenzy; it is the source of extreme stimulation in forms ranging from madness to spiritual ecstasy. Harnessed by will, it can be used for great deeds of action and creativity; divine seed of the self.

World Tree - the central axis of the Nine Worlds that supports all life. (see Axis; Odhinn's steed; Irminsul; Nine Worlds, Yggdrasil).

Wyrd (OE) - (Urdhr ON) the continuum of space, time and events in which the proper results of all actions are manifested.

Ydalir (ON) - (yew dale) Dwelling Hall of the god Ullur (see Ullur).

Yggdrasill (ON) - (steed of the terrible one, ie. Odhinn) the World-Tree that supports the multiverse (see Irminsul, Nine Worlds, World Tree).

Ymir (ON) - (groaner) first Frost-Giant, formed when the heat of Muspellheim met the rime of Niflheim in the void of Ginnungagap melting the ice into drips which quickened with life.

Younger Futhark - the Scandinavian rune system where the number of staves was reduced from 24 (Elder Futhark) to 16 (around the 8th century CE) but the magickal order and combination was kept through integrating the functions of certain runes for multiple meaning.

Zisa - see Cisa.

Book Hoard

Aswynn, Freya. 1990. *The Leaves of Yggdrasil*, Llewellyn Publ.

Crossley-Holland, Kevin. 1980. *The Norse Myths - Gods of the Vikings*, Penguin Books.

Edinger, Edward F. 1974 . *Ego and Archetype* (C.G. Jung's fundamental psychological concepts), Penguin Books.

Elliott, R.W.V. 1959. *Runes: An Introduction*, Manchester University Press.

Ellis Davidson, H.R. 1988. *Myths and Symbols in Pagan Europe, Early Scandinavian and Celtic Religions*, Syracuse University Press.

Faulkes, A.. 1995. *Edda*, Sturluson, S. Trans.

Flowers, Stephen E. 1988. *The Secret of the Runes* (Guido Von List), Edited, Translated by S.E.F. Destiny Books.

Gordon, E.V. 1956. *An Introduction to Old Norse*, Clarendon Press Oxford, 2nd Edition .

Graham-Campell, J. 1989. *The Viking World*, Frances Lincoln Pub. LTD.

Gundarsson, Kveldulf. 1990. *Teutonic Magic - The Magical and Spiritual Practices of the Germanic Peoples*, Llewellyn Publ.

—————————— 1993. *Teutonic Religion - Folk Beliefs and Practices of the Nothern Tradition*, Llewellyn Publ.
—————————— 1993. *Our Troth* (edit. by K.G.), the Ring of Troth.

Hollander, Lee M. 1990. *The Poetic Edda* (translation), University of Texas Press.

Howard, Michael. 1980. *The Magic of The Runes - Their Origins and Occult Power*, Aquarian Press. New Edition - The Mysteries of the Runes 1995 Capall Bann Publishing

Jacobi, Jolande. 1968. *The Psychology of C. G. Jung*, Routledge.

Jung, Carl. 1964.. *Man and his Symbols*, Picador.

King, Bernard. 1993. *The Elements of the Runes*, Element Books.

Magnusson, M & Palsson, H. 1960.
Njal's Saga, Trans. Penguin Books.

Mattingly H. 1970. *Agricola and the Germania* Trans. S. A. Handford. Revised Harmondsworth.

Orchard, Andy. 1997. *Dictionary of Norse Myth and Legend*, Cassell UK.

Osborn & Longland. 1982. *Rune Games*, Penguin Books.

Owen, Francis. 1995. *The Germanic People - Their Origin, Expansion and Culture*, Barnes & Noble Books .

Pennick, Nigel. 1989. *Practical Magic in the Northern Tradition*, Aquarian Press.
_____1992.. *Rune Magic - The History and Magic of Ancient Runic Traditions*, Aquarian Press

Sheldrake, Rupert. 1988. *The Presence of the Past: Morphic Resonance and the Habits of Nature*, Collins.

Stanton, A. 1999. *Ripples in Time - The Anglo-Saxon Runes*, Renewal.

Thorsson, Edred. 1988. *At the Well of Wyrd - A Handbook of Runic Divination*, Samuel Weiser Inc.
_____1984.. *Futhark - A Handbook of Rune Magic*, Samuel Weiser Inc.
_____1992.. *Northern Magic - Mysteries of the Norse, Germans and English*, Llewellyn Publ.
_____1990. *The Nine Doors of Midgard - A Complete Curriculum of Rune Magic*, Llewellyn Publ.

——————1987. *Rune Lore - A Handbook of Esoteric Runology,* Samuel Weiser Inc.

——————1989. *Rune Might - Secret Practices of the German Rune Magicians,* Llewellyn Publ.

——————1989. *A Book of Troth,* Llewellyn Publ.

——————1994.. *The Book of Ogham - The Celtic Tree Oracle,* Llewellyn Publ.

Tyson, Donald. 1989. *Rune Magic,* Llewellyn Publ.

Wodening, E. 1994.. *Wyrd,* Wednesbury School of Theodish Belief.

Wilson, David. M. 1980. *The Northern World - The History and Heritage of Northern Europe,* Thames and Hudson.

Willis, Tony. 1986. *Discover Runes - Understanding and Using the Power of the Runes,* The Aquarian Press.

The Artists

Annika Robertson. Born 1960 in Stockholm, Sweden. Grew up practically outdoors in the Swedish landscape, cultivating interests in natural history and archeology. Studied biology at Uppsala University, Sweden, where she started to develop skills in scientific illustration professionally. After running an Eco-tourism business on the north-west coast of Scotland with her husband, she moved to Adelaide, South Australia, in 1996. She is now pursuing a career of art and illustration and has participated in group exhibitions and regularly submits artwork to juried art shows.

"I really enjoyed doing the illustrations for Rune Rede because they combined my interests in art, archeology and scientific illustration."

Annika can be contacted by email:

AnnikaRobertson@netscape.net

Gregory Griffith. Born in Perth, Western Australia. Developed an interest in organic patterns and textures. Self taught, he became a highly skilled carver in the tribal traditions and an illustrator of fine intricacy. His varied work has been marketed throughout Australia.

Greg can be contacted at:

PO Box 5345 Rockingham Beach WA 6168 Australia

For Further Information on the Northern Tradition and Runes:

Assembly of the Elder Troth (AET) Aust. website:
http://www.homepages.ihug.com.au/~peloquin/index.html

Rune-Net (R-N) Aust. website:
http://www.mackaos.com.au/Rune-Net

FREE DETAILED CATALOGUE

Capall Bann is owned and run by people actively involved in many of the areas in which we publish. A detailed illustrated catalogue is available on request, SAE or International Postal Coupon appreciated. **Titles can be ordered direct from Capall Bann, post free in the** UK (cheque or PO with order) or from good bookshops and specialist outlets.

Do contact us for details on the latest releases at:**Capall Bann Publishing, Freshfilelds,Chieveley, Berks, RG20 8TF.** Titles include:

A Breath Behind Time, Terri Hector
Angels and Goddesses - Celtic Christianity & Paganism, M. Howard
Arthur - The Legend Unveiled, C Johnson & E Lung
Astrology The Inner Eye - A Guide in Everyday Language, E Smith
Auguries and Omens - The Magical Lore of Birds, Yvonne Aburrow
Asyniur - Womens Mysteries in the Northern Tradition, S McGrath
Beginnings - Geomancy, Builder's Rites & Electional Astrology in the
        European Tradition, Nigel Pennick
Between Earth and Sky, Julia Day
Book of the Veil , Peter Paddon
Caer Sidhe - Celtic Astrology and Astronomy, Michael Bayley
Call of the Horned Piper, Nigel Jackson
Cat's Company, Ann Walker
Celtic Faery Shamanism, Catrin James
Celtic Lore & Druidic Ritual, Rhiannon Ryall
Celtic Sacrifice - Pre Christian Ritual & Religion, Marion Pearce
Celtic Saints and the Glastonbury Zodiac, Mary Caine
Circle and the Square, Jack Gale
Compleat Vampyre - The Vampyre Shaman, Nigel Jackson
Creating Form From the Mist - The Wisdom of Women in Celtic Myth and
        Culture, Lynne Sinclair-Wood
Crystal Clear - A Guide to Quartz Crystal, Jennifer Dent
Crystal Doorways, Simon & Sue Lilly
Crossing the Borderlines - Guising, Masking & Ritual Animal Disguise in the
        European Tradition, Nigel Pennick
Dragons of the West, Nigel Pennick
Earth Dance - A Year of Pagan Rituals, Jan Brodic
Earth Harmony - Places of Power, Holiness & Healing, Nigel Pennick
Earth Magic, Margaret McArthur
The Eildon Tree Romany Language & Lore, Achael Hoadley
Enchanted Forest - The Magical Lore of Trees, Yvonne Aburrow